SHERWOOD ANDERSON

In the same series:

(continued on page 134)

MODERN LITERATURE MONOGRAPHS
GENERAL EDITOR: Lina Mainiero

SHERWOOD ANDERSON

Welford Dunaway Taylor

FREDERICK UNGAR PUBLISHING CO.
NEW YORK

Library of Congress Cataloging in Publication Data

Taylor, Welford Dunaway.
  Sherwood Anderson.

  (Modern literature monographs)
  Bibliography: p.
  Includes index.
    1. Anderson, Sherwood, 1876–1941—Criticism and
interpretation.
PS3501.N4Z857   813'.5'2   77-6948
ISBN 0-8044-2862-2

For Eleanor Anderson, Amy Nyholm,
and Virginia Welford Taylor,
with love to all

115507

Contents

Chronology

1876: Sherwood Anderson born to Irwin and Emma Smith Anderson in Camden, Ohio, on 13 September.

1884: Anderson family moves to Clyde, Ohio; for twelve years Sherwood works at odd jobs and attends school sporadically.

1895: Emma Smith Anderson dies.

1896–98: Sherwood works as a laborer in Chicago.

1898–99: Serves in the Spanish-American War.

1900: Completes senior year of high school at Wittenburg Academy.

1900–06: Works as advertiser in Chicago; publishes numerous articles in *Agricultural Advertising*.

1904: Marries Cornelia Lane of Toledo, Ohio, on 16 May.

1906: Moves to Cleveland to become president of United Factories Company.

1907: Moves to Elyria, Ohio, to head mail-order paint business.

1912: Leaves Elyria office, dazed, on morning of 28 November; is found in Cleveland on 1 December and hospitalized.

1913–15: Returns to Chicago and advertising; meets various figures of Chicago Renaissance.

1916: Obtains final divorce from Cornelia on 27 July; marries Tennessee Mitchell on 31 July; publishes *Windy McPherson's Son* (first novel).

1917:   Publishes *Marching Men.*

1919:   Publishes *Winesburg, Ohio.*

1921:   Publishes *Poor White*; spends three months in Europe, meets Gertrude Stein; wins *Dial* award; publishes *Triumph of the Egg.*

1922:   Leaves Chicago and advertising permanently; separates from Tennessee; meets Elizabeth Prall in New York.

1923:   Publishes *Many Marriages* and *Horses and Men*; lives in Reno, Nevada, establishing residence for divorce.

1924:   Divorces Tennessee; marries Elizabeth Prall; moves to New Orleans; publishes *A Story Teller's Story* (first autobiographical book).

1925:   Goes on lecture tour; vacations in Troutdale, Virginia; publishes *Dark Laughter*; purchases Ripshin Farm, near Troutdale.

1927:   Buys *Marion Democrat* and *Smyth County News*, weekly newspapers in Marion, Virginia.

1928:   Meets Eleanor Copenhaver of Marion.

1929:   Publishes *Hello Towns!*; separates from Elizabeth Prall.

1930:   Visits southern mills, views labor problems with Eleanor Copenhaver.

1931:   Publishes *Perhaps Women.*

1932:   Divorces Elizabeth Prall; lectures; attends pacifist rally in Amsterdam.

1933:   Marries Eleanor Copenhaver; publishes *Death in the Woods.*

1936:   Publishes *Kit Brandon* (final novel).

1940:   Publishes *Home Town.*

1941:   Dies in Colon, Panama, of peritonitis on 8 March.

SHERWOOD ANDERSON

1

American Adventure

In observing that "one of the most characteristic things about American life is our isolation from one another,"[1] Sherwood Anderson reiterated the sense of alienation that has become a theme of much twentieth-century American literature. He could make such a statement with more authority than many contemporary writers. Having grown up in small midwestern towns in the last quarter of the nineteenth century, he had seen quiet villages of farmers and tradesmen disrupted by the advent of factories with machines that could produce more goods in less time than ever before. He had witnessed an erosion of close human relationships as one man competed with another for financial success and positions of authority. Those who were most assertive and who showed the least regard for the concerns of others and for human values in general he called "grotesques."

The changes wrought by industrialism were not the only cause of alienation. As Anderson made wide-ranging travels through the United States, first as a businessman, then as a writer, he came to recognize a pronounced diversity in the beliefs and loyalties of the people. "We have no common religion, no common love of the land,"[2] he concluded. As a kindly, outgoing man who felt a strong emotional attraction to people and a concern for the well-being of his country, Anderson felt as repelled by this sense of separateness as by the growing emphasis upon materialism and the corresponding decline in human values.

"People are brought close to each other through some common passion,"[3] he maintained. Although he was forty when he published his first work of fiction, he strove for the next twenty-five years to express the problem of dehumanization in America and to search for the "common passion" by which Americans might be drawn closer together. This quest is a central issue in both his work and life.

Sherwood Berton Anderson was born on September 13, 1876, in Camden, Ohio, a small midwestern town he remembered as "intimate and close."[4] He was the third of seven children born to Emma Smith and Irwin McLain Anderson. Though both parents influenced his personality decisively and appear frequently in his fictional and autobiographical writings, his father was especially dominant.

Sherwood once described the elder Anderson as an "improvident fellow,"[5] and this evaluation seems fair. Irwin painted houses and signs, hung wallpaper and made harnesses; but he worked at nothing for very long. His abiding interests were drinking, playing the cornet in town bands (on one occasion with Warren G. Harding),[6] and storytelling. His favorite subjects for tales were his Civil War experiences (he had served in the Union army as a private), and he cut a dandy figure at patriotic celebrations when he donned the fancy uniform of the Grand Army of the Republic, a Civil War veterans' organization.

Sherwood felt toward his father a mixture of love and resentment. He was justified in seeing Irwin as a great striker of poses, a braggart, and something of a ne'er-do-well. The numerous father characters who strut and lie their way through the pages of Sherwood's early fiction are recognizable representations of Irwin. But the son gradually became more sympathetic toward his father's prevarications, for he came to recognize the same inclination in himself. He, no less than Irwin, functioned not in a real world, but in one created out of his own imagination; and as this realization grew, his portrayal of his father changed. In *A Story Teller's Story* (1924), Sherwood's eighth book, Irwin is pictured as a charming and quick-witted raconteur.

Less is known of Emma Smith Anderson. Her German ancestry can be traced; a few facts of her midwestern girlhood have been discovered; a small amount is known of her life as the hard-working wife of a shiftless husband. These meager facts are overshadowed by Sherwood's accounts. Though certainly tinged with imagination, his portraits of Emma are vivid and sympathetic. He remembered her as "dark, beautiful and somewhat mysterious,"[7] and he liked to say that she was Italian, which was untrue. More accurate, perhaps, was his memory of her taking in washing to help support the family and "coming into our little frame house on a winter day after hanging a wash out on a line . . . the look of patient suffering on her face."[8] He acknowledged something of her influence when, in the dedication of *Winesburg, Ohio* (1919), his finest book, he states that her "keen observations on the life about her first awoke in me the hunger to see beneath the surface of lives."

About 1884, Irwin Anderson moved his family to Clyde, the northwestern Ohio town usually associated with Sherwood's youth. Clyde was the place Sherwood remembered best from the various localities he had known as a boy; it inspired the fictional Winesburg and similar towns in his novels and stories. It awak-

ened in him a lifelong love of the small, quiet towns
that had existed before the coming of the machines
and factories.

There were times in Clyde when he enjoyed such
pleasures as playing in a cave where he and his friends
acted out scenes from James Fenimore Cooper's
Leather-Stocking Tales. But most of his time was spent
working, and he held so many jobs that he earned
the name Jobby. These chores often conflicted with
his schooling. He was frequently absent, and formal
education came to mean little to him. He preferred to
borrow interesting books from the school principal's
private library, and he read whenever he could find
the time.

Nonacademic life proved a broad education, however. After his mother's death in 1895 (Sherwood was
now eighteen), he drifted to Chicago, where he worked
as a laborer in a warehouse and attempted a course
in business mathematics. In 1898 he enlisted for service
in Cuba. As a soldier in the Spanish-American War,
his role was more quixotic than heroic. Never getting
to the front, he spent the majority of his service time
training and reading. He must have regarded the
heroes' welcome given his company in Clyde a year
later with a mixed sense of pride and ludicrousness.

Not long after he returned from Cuba, Anderson
decided to join his brother Karl in Springfield, Ohio,
to attend Wittenburg Academy. During the 1899–1900
term he completed his senior year of high school with
distinguished marks and delivered an oration at com-
mencement exercises. The year at Wittenburg proved
important to his development and to his fortunes.
Not only did it give structure to his intellectual interests; it provided an opportunity for associating with
people of talent and accomplishment. Among the
teachers, editors, and artists who shared lodgings with
the Anderson brothers was Marco Morrow, an adver-

tising executive from Chicago. He and Sherwood formed a lasting friendship, and three months after graduation Sherwood was in Chicago to take a job in advertising that Morrow had made possible.

This initial involvement with advertising lasted four years. But during the next two decades he would drift in and out of this vocation whenever he needed money. He soon came to see in advertising much slickness and insincerity, two characteristics he denounced throughout his life. Taking Anderson's own disparaging assessment at face value, critics have tended to think of this experience as a painful and unproductive episode in his development. It must be remembered, however, that advertising first gave him the stimulus to write and publish.

In addition to producing routine copy, he soon began publishing short feature articles in *Agricultural Advertising*. These appeared frequently in 1903 and 1904, and they revealed a writer who perceived vivid details in the commonplace aspects of farming, which writers for such publications did not usually notice. The imaginative flair that was to mark the later creative work can be discerned in these articles.

Still, the idea of writing for the sole purpose of increasing the volume of business of his clients never sat comfortably with Sherwood. When Cyrus Curtis, publisher of the *Saturday Evening Post,* offered him a position on that magazine, he refused because he knew he would be expected to write articles that glorified business.

On May 16, 1904, Sherwood married Cornelia Lane of Toledo, Ohio, a woman with whom he contrasted in several ways. She was a graduate of Western Reserve University and had traveled and studied in Europe. As the daughter of a wealthy shoe wholesaler, she represented the secure mercantile class to a husband who was beginning to question the business practices he had observed. Nevertheless, Sherwood himself soon moved further into business by assuming the presidency of the United Factories Company of Cleveland in 1906.

From this time until late 1912, he remained in the business world. At times he succeeded; at other times he failed. As the years wore on, his responsibilities grew. Three children were born, in 1907, 1908, and 1911. In 1907 he moved to Elyria, Ohio, and started the Anderson Manufacturing Company, a mail-order house that marketed an inexpensive roof coating. He joined the country club and learned to play golf. Still, as his participation in the world of business increased, so did his questionings of the profit motive and the ruthless competition upon which American business was founded.

At the same time, his interest in reading and the urge to write grew steadily. Though it is difficult to determine when writing became his active avocation, Cornelia recalled that he eagerly discussed books in meetings of a literary discussion group formed in Elyria in 1910 and that he occasionally stayed up all night writing. She also noted that "Sherwood never went on a bus or anywhere that he didn't come home with the life story of some acquaintance."[9]

The more he read and attempted to write, the more attractive he found the role of the writer. Writing, it seemed to Sherwood, was relatively free from the slickness, insincerity, and materialism that characterized American business practices. Yet, attractive as a writing career seemed, his responsibilities to his business were various and demanding. For a long time he tried to fulfill obligations both to his vocation and to his burgeoning literary interests. But each seemed to work against the other, and gradually his health was threatened. Finally, on the morning of November 28, 1912, he came to the office of the Anderson Manufacturing Company looking haggard and preoccupied. He began speaking incoherently and left. Four days later he was found in Cleveland, dazed and exhausted, and was committed to a hospital there. He never returned to his business.

By early February, 1913, he was again established in Chicago, working once more for an advertising agency, but this time attempting to publish the manuscripts of two novels he had brought with him.

Sherwood often recounted the story of how he walked out of his business office into a literary career, thus making the episode the single best known fact of his life. No two of these accounts are identical, as each reflects the characteristic shadings of his imagination and his apparent desire to make his action legendary. However the story is altered, it is clear that the incident was decisive. Subsequently, his commitment to art was total. This is not to say that he was able to ignore business completely. He worked sporadically in advertising for almost ten more years; but he managed to continue writing. Some of his finest work was written in this decade. For instance, he wrote "I'm A Fool," one of his most successful short stories, while he was supposedly producing an advertisement for a gasoline-engine company.

In his own way, Sherwood always felt a strong sense of responsibility toward his wife and children, and in April, 1913, he brought them from Elyria to live near Chicago. Thinking that he had found a publisher for one of his novels, he moved the entire family to the Ozarks for the winter of 1913 and 1914. This proved a strain for everyone concerned. The novel was not published, and money became extremely scarce. By the end of the experience he and Cornelia had decided to divorce.

Many have interpreted Sherwood Anderson's divorce as a heartless abandonment of family responsibilities for a selfish goal. This allegation is discounted by the fact that he always maintained close contact with Cornelia and the children and, when possible, helped with their education and careers. It is true that he contributed very little money in the early years after the separation. He was struggling to exist and to write, and he never realized large sums from his work. It is also true that Cornelia had to bear the day-to-day responsibilities of rearing the children and that she taught school until retirement. However, she freely admitted that the decision to end the marriage was as difficult for Sherwood as it was for her, and one infers that she was not unhappy about the divorce. "The step he took in giving up his family was not an easy one," she recalled years later, "but I still think he did the right thing. . . . I am a much better person for having known him."[10]

This was an exciting time for an aspiring writer to be in Chicago. At the time of Anderson's arrival in early 1913, the innovative work of a small group of young midwestern poets, novelists, and editors was beginning to make an impact upon national letters. Members of the group were progressive in their approach to literature, their political opinions, and their life styles. They disliked, for instance, the strict verse forms and prudish taste of the poetry that appeared in popular magazines. Many published their work in *Poetry* magazine or in the *Little Review,* two little magazines founded in Chicago in 1912 and 1914 that published the contributions of avant-garde authors.

Anderson knew most of the prominent figures of the movement and was encouraged by them. He lived in the same building with Floyd Dell and Marjorie Curry, who heard him read his manuscripts and aided him in finding a publisher. He read for the first time new and controversial authors such as Gertrude Stein.

He heard Carl Sandburg play his guitar and recite his poems at parties, and he spent an entire night reading Edgar Lee Masters's new collection of poems, *Spoon River Anthology* (1915).

One of the benefits of associating with the Chicago group was that he met Tennessee Mitchell. A teacher of piano and dancing, and later a sculptor, Tennessee Mitchell had become friends of both Sherwood and Cornelia soon after they arrived in Chicago. She was named for the famous suffragist and libertarian Tennessee Claflin, and she was as liberated as the original Tennessee. She was known for her flamboyant dress and for frankness and loyalty to her friends. She and Sherwood were married on July 31, 1916, just four days after his divorce from Cornelia became final. Again, Cornelia showed understanding. Sherwood and Tennessee visited with her and the children on their wedding trip, and remained good friends thereafter.

Cornelia later remarked to Sherwood that "evidently marriages are but cycles."[11] In so saying, she was commenting not only on her own marriage but also on Sherwood's marriage to Tennessee. The latter union lasted from 1916 until 1924, and it proved to be the most important period in his artistic development. The nature of their relationship was only one of several indications that he was attempting to adopt the free and somewhat daring ways of the Chicago group. He and Tennessee occupied separate apartments, and each earned a living independently. By mutual agreement each came and went at will and was not answerable to the other in matters of fidelity and obedience.

Following the publication of his first book, *Windy McPherson's Son* (1916), Anderson produced steadily and prolifically for the next several years. Though this first novel and a second, *Marching Men*

(1917), sold poorly, they earned favorable notices from prestigious reviewers. A rather lame attempt at poetry, *Mid-American Chants* (1918), was more than compensated for by *Poor White* (1921), his finest novel. It soon became obvious, however, that Anderson's forte was the short story. After publishing several individual stories in such progressive magazines as *Masses* and *Seven Arts*—"little highbrow magazines,"[12] as he called them—he published three collections in rapid succession: *Winesburg, Ohio* (1919), *The Triumph of the Egg* (1921), and *Horses and Men* (1923).

The short stories, more than any other literary mode, established Sherwood Anderson's reputation as a major influence in American literature. Edward J. O'Brien, editor of *The Best Short Stories*, an annual anthology, included Anderson selections for many years, and dedicated the 1920 volume to him. In 1921, Sherwood won the *Dial* award as the most promising writer of the year.

Even during these active years of publishing and generally favorable critical reception, Anderson continued to work in advertising. Not until 1922 was he able to leave it permanently. As he left advertising, he realized that his marriage to Tennessee was coming to the point of severance. Although he had often expressed pleasure in being with her, there is some indication that he never attained the closeness he would have liked. "I never go to Tennessee's house but I go a little timidly, questioning," he confessed. "I want to know how I am to be received."[13]

It is likely that the unorthodox residential arrangement that seemed so attractive in the beginning contributed to the divisiveness. Having attempted in his fiction to point out the walls that separated individuals from each other and to stress the importance of close communication among people, Sherwood was not one who could accept such alienation in his own marriage. Moreover, Tennessee had become, untaught, a fairly accomplished sculptor, and Sherwood began to feel he was in competition with her.

Anderson was by nature a wanderer, and when he found himself becoming enveloped by unpleasant circumstances, his wanderlust usually proved irresistible. In 1922, he went to New Orleans and then to New York City. There he met Elizabeth Prall, manager of the Doubleday-Doran bookstore, and soon fell in love with her. While waiting for his divorce to come through, he published *Many Marriages* (1923), a novel that frankly discusses the emptiness that lies at the core of marriage in the modern world and reflects his own uncertainties as to what constitutes the ideal marriage.

In 1924, the year of his marriage to Elizabeth Prall, he published *A Story Teller's Story*, an autobiographical novel. Bearing many marks of middle age, it is, on the whole, a fond memory of the author's youth; but it offers more favorable reflection upon the past than promise for the future. Anderson appeared, however, to be facing pleasant prospects. He was taking a new bride, and was planning a fresh start in New Orleans.

Though he soon became disappointed with the New Orleans climate and repelled by the "half-artists"[14] of the French Quarter, he made friends with the architect William Spratling and with the young Mississippi writer William Faulkner, whose first novel, *Soldier's Pay* (1926), he helped get published. In the spring of 1925, on the advice of a friend, he left New Orleans to spend what he intended as a holiday in the mountains of southwestern Virginia, near Marion. Finding the people unusually friendly and the country quiet and lovely, he soon began thinking of settling there.

In the autumn of 1925, *Dark Laughter* was pub-

lished. Before the end of the year this novel had gone
through several printings and had yielded more than
eight thousand dollars in royalties, a greater sum than
he had realized from any prior book. In 1926, he and
Elizabeth purchased a tract of land near Troutdale,
Virginia, and began work on Ripshin, an imposing
country house designed by William Spratling.

In many ways, this turn of events was ironic. *Dark
Laughter* seems an unlikely Anderson book to have
become a bestseller. Like *Many Marriages*, it deals
more with disillusionment over the bankruptcy of
modern marriage, and American social institutions in
general, than it does with any positive alternatives.
The dark laughter of the title is the natural, primitive mirth of the blacks that echoes throughout the
book. It indicates an intuitive appreciation for human impulses with which the middle-class white
American had lost touch.

Sherwood hoped that his move to a less compli-
cated environment would effect positive changes in
his own life. The results, at least initially, were not
so decisive.

In 1926, Horace Liveright, Sherwood's publisher,
had offered him one hundred dollars a week for five
years, with the understanding that he write about one
book per year. With this amount, plus income from
Dark Laughter, and from lecturing, he would be able
to build his house and to live free from financial
worries. But new problems emerged. To fulfill his
commitment, he tried desperately to write and failed
repeatedly. Though he blamed this inhibition on the
newly acquired trappings of the gentleman farmer
and the security offered by the Liveright subsidy, there
were deeper reasons. One was certainly the obligation
to produce. He had never been able to force himself
to write; for him words had to flow naturally. In his
early fifties now, Sherwood realized that he had al-

ready told many times the stories of his youth, his family, his struggle to become a writer, and the frustrations of the sensitive artist trying to function in an impersonal, materialistic society. The move to Virginia might provide relief from these conditions.

Sherwood came to doubt whether he could ever write again, and this problem weighed more heavily upon him than has been supposed. Elizabeth Prall recalled that he became so desperate that one day as he was driving with her he suddenly swerved the car off a mountain road, as if attempting to kill the both of them.[15] (Fortunately, the car did not overturn.)

Sherwood was later to summarize this frustrating period by admitting, "I was associating altogether too much with one Sherwood Anderson. I never grew so tired of a man in my life."[16] This statement was characteristic of Anderson: it was an admission that by internalizing his own problems and by doting on his failures he had become grotesque—separated from his fellow man and thus unable to communicate with himself.

In the fall of 1927, however, the situation changed. Sherwood learned by chance that the two local newspapers, the *Smyth County News* (Republican) and the *Marion Democrat* (Democratic) were for sale. Shortly thereafter, he became owner, editor, publisher, and, for a time, principal writer for these weeklies. The subjects of Sherwood's newspaper columns indicate that the focus of his attention had changed from personal concerns to those of a town of four thousand and the rural counties surrounding it. Not only was he writing actively again; he was once more in a small town, which in many ways resembled the pleasant communities he had known as a boy.

A strong element of personal conflict remained, however. Early in 1929, Sherwood offered to send Elizabeth to California for a visit with her family; she eagerly accepted. A few days after arriving, she received a letter from him containing the simple statement, "I just wish you would not come back."[17] She never saw him again.

It appears difficult to reconcile this shocking and unexpected action with the relatively honorable manner in which the two former marriages were terminated, and with the genial attitude that Sherwood displayed in his works and to his many friends. He did, however, attempt an explanation more than a year after Elizabeth had left. All three wives, he maintained,

. . . lost courage and wouldn't adventure any more.

Wanting to sit secure behind walls.

Odd, isn't it, but that Tennessee came the nearest? She saw the thing—taking life so, with gusto, to the last drop.

I used to take her sometimes to the very door [of new adventures], put her hand on the doorknob, but she always ran away like a frightened child.[18]

Although Sherwood never specified what he meant by "adventuring," his comment makes clear that he blamed Cornelia, Tennessee, and Elizabeth for looking to him primarily for security. This explanation seems plausible, if not pardonable. He had taken considerable risks in leaving business to write. He had taken a risk when he left advertising entirely in 1922, and a greater risk when he bought the Marion newspapers in 1927. He had chosen the uncertainty of writing what and as he pleased over Horace Liveright's offer of a regular income for a specified number of novels. Like all adventurers, he was threatened by security.

Publishing the newspapers was an example of this spirit of adventure. Sherwood had had no experience in journalism. But from his first issue he spoke to his readers in an informal, familiar, and often humorous voice that indicated his adeptness in adjusting to new situations. In 1929 he collected a large number of columns from his first year of journalistic writing into a volume, *Hello Towns!* Within a few months, however, he began turning his attention to some of the larger issues affecting not only south-western Virginia but the south in general.

In late October, 1929, the American stock market plummeted. Like many other communities, Marion suffered from the great depression that followed. Having ceded most of the responsibilities of running the newspapers to his son, Robert Lane Anderson, Sherwood now spent a great deal of time traveling about the south, observing conditions and helping in what ways he could.

In 1928, he had met Eleanor Copenhaver, daughter of a leading Marion family, who was actively interested in the plight of the southern working girl. After his separation from Elizabeth in early 1929, he came to know Eleanor better. She began to interest him in her work, and he frequently visited southern factories with her. From these trips came *Perhaps Women* (1931), a series of vivid impressions of modern working girls, expressed in prose essays. These demonstrate that Sherwood's interests had extended beyond the precincts of Marion and nearby areas.

More importantly, it was obvious that Sherwood had begun to realize some specific possibilities within his own Virginia locale that offered a way to regain some of the human qualities he believed Americans had lost. For instance, the pressure for collective bargaining was beginning to be felt in the southern labor market. He made speeches supporting the demands of striking textile workers in Danville, Virginia, and he wrote in defense of deprived coal miners in Harlan County, Kentucky.

Labor problems, however, represented but a fraction of America's needs at this time. A plummeting of

prices on Wall Street which, between October 23 and
mid-November, 1929 had resulted in thirty billion
dollars in losses, had heralded the most crippling
economic depression the country had ever experienced.
Sherwood saw the millions of unemployed workers,
ruined businesses and depleted banks as reflecting
the basic inequities of American capitalism. At the
time of the stock market collapse, the wealthiest five
percent of the American population was making one-
third of the entire personal income in the country; the
27,500 wealthiest Americans had as much money as
the twelve million poorest.[19] Because capitalism had
created this grossly inequitable distribution of wealth,
Sherwood and many other disillusioned Americans
looked about for alternatives to this system. For a time
Sherwood flirted with Marxism, and attended the
World Congress Against War in Amsterdam in 1932.[20]
Soon becoming disillusioned with communism, however, he endeavored to dissociate himself from it.

   In 1933, he entered the most stable and satisfying
period of his life. Its beginning was marked by his
marriage to Eleanor Copenhaver in July, 1933. She
was some twenty years his junior, and she took an enthusiastic part in the social causes that concerned him.
She had attended the University of Richmond and
Columbia and had held a national post in the
Y.W.C.A. for several years before the marriage. She
represented both the southern aristocratic tradition
and a commitment to social reform for the under-
privileged.

   Sherwood was pleased to be accepted by the
Copenhaver family, and by the time of his marriage
he was becoming enthusiastic about the new Roosevelt administration which had come into office in
March, 1933. He and Eleanor knew personally some
of the people who were to develop the New Deal. As
he embarked upon a new marriage, he was thus heart-

ened by a sense of domestic stability and by a feeling of confidence for the future of the country. Although he had berated his former wives for not being adventurous, he freely admitted his appreciation for having finally found a sense of solidity.

Since the mid-1920s, his detractors had charged that his career as a fiction writer was finished. However, "Brother Death" and "Death in the Woods," from *Death in the Woods, and Other Stories* (1933), are perhaps the two finest stories he ever wrote. *Kit Brandon* (1936) demonstrated that he could still write successful novels; and *Plays: Winesburg and Others* (1937), his only volume of dramas, reveals his consistent interest in experimenting with new literary forms.

During the last year of his life he worked on his *Memoirs*. This final statement, published the year after his death, is that of a generally contented man, "lucky to have been born in America in what well may turn out to have been America's happiest period."[21] It is pervaded by a sense of gratitude for his family, his small-town boyhood, and the hard work he had done. Though he realized that he had many detractors as well as defenders, he was aware that *Winesburg, Ohio* was an American classic. With characteristic modesty, however, he summarized his career by stating the belief that he was "only a minor figure."[22]

While the *Memoirs* suggest a sense of having come to the end of his life, there are many passages that indicate continuing enjoyment of life. In February, 1941, he set out with Eleanor for his first trip to South America. He had been given semiofficial sanction by the State Department to study life in South American towns, and *Reader's Digest* had promised to publish a series of stories he planned to write. On the eve of his departure, he was feted at a cocktail party

in New York and swallowed the toothpick from a
martini olive. This penetrated his intestines, and peritonitis developed. Eight days later he died at Colon,
Panama.

The nature of Anderson's demise seems to epito-
mize his life and career. He believed that life was not
measured by the birth and death of individual people;
it was rather a broad sweep of human history, forever
ongoing, forever changing. Having spent a lifetime
experiencing and interpreting contemporary life, he
died in the process of exploring it still further. Both
in its beautiful and revolting manifestations, life for
Sherwood Anderson remained to the end a limitless
source of fascination and a constant challenge for intense participation as an artist. This fact he summarized when he wrote the epitaph that adorns his
tombstone: "Life, not death, is the great adventure."

2

Re-inventing the American Soul

The fictional village of Winesburg, Ohio, is a cross-
roads, where humanity and time converge. Many of
the residents who appear in the twenty-two *Winesburg,
Ohio* stories are natives; many have gravitated to the
town from other parts of America, seeking escape
or a new life. The life strands of both natives and
newcomers are interwoven into a fabric of village life.
By their dreams, frustrations, and relationship to
society, the Winesburg citizenry symbolize Anderson's
view of the condition of American life in the first
quarter of the twentieth century.

Winesburg, Ohio also represents a melding of
two time periods. Though narrated in the mid-1910s,
it is set in the post-Civil War period—in that space
between Appomattox and the coming of the industrial
boom to the small towns of the midwest. The external
characteristics of the buildings and streets of Winesburg are not presented in fine detail, but the impression is communicated of a quiet country village, the
sort that constituted the midwestern United States
during the last quarter of the nineteenth century.

As narrator of the stories, Anderson himself ex-
emplifies both youth and old age. In the opening
sketch, "The Book of the Grotesque," he tells of his
association with an aged writer, the author of a volume
entitled *The Book of the Grotesque*, part of which

Anderson quotes. Then, in "Hands," the second *Winesburg* selection, Anderson introduces a youthful character named George Willard, who figures in all but two of the subsequent stories. As a reporter for the town newspaper, and an aspiring writer intent on learning about life through his repeated intimate contacts with the inhabitants of Winesburg, George is a reflection of the younger persona of Sherwood Anderson.

The *Winesburg* stories were completed in 1916, the year Anderson turned forty. Three years before he had rejected a business career to become a writer, but thus far his efforts had resulted in only two small stories published in magazines. *Winesburg, Ohio* evolved from a period of loneliness, because of his separation from Cornelia, and unhappiness at having to earn a living by writing advertising copy. Living alone on the third floor of a rooming house in downtown Chicago, he experienced the city as being cold and impersonal.

Grotesques

"The Book of the Grotesque" is an attempt to explain the causes of alienation and to suggest ways of overcoming its effects. Part of this explanation is stated in the words of an old writer, who resembles Anderson in several respects. Like Anderson, the old man was once a loving, outgoing individual who in his youth had known many people "in a peculiarly intimate way." Gradually he has become separated from them and now lives alone in a single room. The old man has even had his bed elevated (as Anderson had), in order that he might look out of his window and thus feel less isolated from the world.

One night the old man lay on the raised bed half

asleep, half awake, and pondered his former friends. It suddenly occurred to him that they had all been transformed into grotesques—estranged people whose minds and lives had become distorted. In his perception of the word, however, not all grotesques were horrible; "some were amusing, some almost beautiful."

The old man climbed down from his bed and wrote a book about those grotesques that particularly interested him. Although the book was never published, Anderson claims to have seen it. He says that it made "an indelible impression" on his mind and that by remembering it he has "been able to understand many people and things [he] was never able to understand before."

Anderson summarizes the unnamed old man's definition of grotesqueness as follows:

. . . In the beginning when the world was young there were a great many thoughts but no such thing as a truth. Man made the truths himself and each truth was a composite of a great many vague thoughts. All about in the world were the truths and they were all beautiful.

. . . I will not try to tell you all of them. There was the truth of virginity and the truth of passion, the truth of wealth and of poverty, of thrift and of profligacy, of carelessness and of abandon.

And then the people came along. Each as he appeared snatched up one of the truths and some who were quite strong snatched up a dozen of them.

It was the truths that made the people grotesques. The old man had quite an elaborate theory concerning the matter. It was his notion that the moment one of the people took one of the truths to himself, called it his truth, and tried to live his life by it, he became a grotesque and the truth he embraced became a falsehood.

Anderson's "Book of the Grotesque" should be seen as a controlling piece for the twenty-one stories that follow, for each contains a character in which grotesqueness is manifest. Some of these people are revolting, some are amusing, some are beautiful—but all are presented by Anderson with feeling and sympathy.

Jesse Bentley is perhaps the most deluded and overbearing of the grotesques in the town of Winesburg. He is the protagonist of "Godliness," the longest of the stories, the title of which identifies the particular truth he has seized, called his own, and become perverted by.

Bentley's training for the Presbyterian ministry had been interrupted by the Civil War. Because all his brothers had been killed in this conflict, he felt obligated to help his father run the family farm. He by no means forgot his Presbyterian zeal, however, and his early success in farming convinced him that it was God's will that he expand his lands and fortune. He married soon after the war. On the day that his wife delivered their only child, he went into his fields and admonished God: "Create in me another Jesse, like that one of old, to rule over men and to be the father of sons who shall be rulers!"

Anderson observes that "like a thousand other strong men who have come into the world here in America in these later times, Jesse was but half strong. He could master others but could not master himself." He is of course crushed to learn that the child is a girl, and he can never bring himself to love her.

Unloved by her father, and by her mother, who has been dominated by Jesse too long to show love, the little girl is often neglected. She becomes retiring and uncommunicative. When her mother dies, Jesse sends her to Winesburg to board with friends and attend high school. Still yearning to be loved, she eventually makes advances toward Tom Hardy, son of the family with whom she is living. Fearing that she is pregnant, she marries him. Though her fears of pregnancy prove false, she later gives birth to a son, David. But, having never known real affection herself, she is unable to show it to the boy. She becomes increasingly withdrawn and occasionally violent. Jesse takes the boy to the farm to live with him.

Old Jesse, who has accumulated several farms through the years and is more obsessed with wealth than ever, senses that finally God's preordained plan is about to be fulfilled. The godliness he had known as a divinity student has been perverted into greed for money, land, and succeeding generations of powerful men. His grandson, who bears the name of the legendary founder of Israel, will beget this race.

The final section of the four-part story is called "Terror."[1] By now old Jesse's warped sense of divine sanction for his selfish schemes has become a mania. Seeking a clear sign of approval from God, he carries David and a tiny lamb to a quiet place in a forest on one of his farms. He prepares to slaughter the animal, hoping to call forth the divine presence. David is of course terrified and runs away. Old Jesse chases after him. The boy takes out a slingshot and flings a stone at the old man, which strikes him squarely. David then flees and is never heard from again in Winesburg.

By having the final scene suggest the Old Testament story of the boy David's slaying of the Philistine giant Goliath, Anderson achieves both forceful drama and biting irony. Old Jesse's grotesque perversion of the words of the scriptures is defeated in a manner suggested in the Old Testament.

In a broader sense, the story is a commentary upon the puritan work ethic. Like many midwestern families in Anderson's fiction, the Bentleys had come from the eastern seaboard, bringing with them respect for the traditional virtues of hard work and thrift. Anderson finds such virtues suspect because they so easily lead people self-righteously into mate-

rialism and avarice. The defeat of Jesse Bentley's perverted scheme indicates that Anderson saw destruction as the ultimate result of grotesqueness that takes
the form of selfish aggression.

Although the explanation of the grotesques in
"The Book of the Grotesque" is one of the most
effective passages in *Winesburg, Ohio*, it is limited—
the term subsumes only the person who has become
grotesque by laying claim to a "truth" that distorts
him. This implies that all grotesques are grasping,
assertive people and that the motives of grotesques
are basically selfish. Yet, in the same section, Anderson
speaks of those who are "amusing" and "almost beautiful." Neither condition suggests the aggressiveness of
the egotistical grotesques.

"Adventure," the story of Alice Hindman, a
non-aggressive grotesque, contains the elements of a
sentimental melodrama. As a girl of sixteen, Alice had
made love with Ned Curry, a writer for the *Winesburg Eagle*. He later went to Cleveland to find a
better job, promising to return and marry her. At
the time the story takes place, she is twenty-seven,
and he has never returned.

In Anderson's treatment, however, Alice's story
has little resemblance to a sentimental account of a
country maiden whose lover is seduced by the evils
of the city. It is, rather, a penetrating psychological
study. Recalling the definition of grotesqueness, one
recognizes that the "truth," or idea, that Alice has
seized on is a concept of romantic love, derived out
of the fantasies she weaves around her brief affair.

Anderson in no sense implies that Alice is selfish
in indulging her inclination. Indeed he seems to sym-
pathize with her. He is rather attempting to demonstrate that when fantasizing obscures one's ability to
perceive reality, the results can be catastrophic.

Alice's memory of physical love is the seed of a dream of Ned's return. Over a period of eleven years, the loneliness increases—and ultimately becomes desperation. One rainy night, this desperation becomes more than she can bear. She runs, naked, from her house through the streets of Winesburg.

Alice's bizarre action is a reckless attempt to experience the imaginary romantic adventure that has engrossed her. Sadly, it will probably be the only adventure she will ever know. Her dreams of marriage to Ned Curry make her uneasy with other men; it is unlikely that she can ever feel otherwise. Apparently, however, she has realized something useful from her actions: later, as she lies sobbing on her bed, she begins "trying to force herself to face bravely the fact that many people must live and die alone, even in Winesburg." The implication is that although she may never know love, she is at least now able to relinquish her tightly held fantasy.

Another grotesque who elicits sympathy from the reader is Dr. Reefy, one of two physicians who live in Winesburg. He appears in two stories, "Paper Pills" and "Death."

"Paper Pills" is a haunting story about the contrast that can exist between appearance and reality. Dr. Reefy is a seemingly ugly old man, with an extraordinarily large nose and huge hands with knuckles like gnarled apples. He wears a threadbare suit. But Anderson quickly adds that "in Dr. Reefy there were the seeds of something very fine." For years he has sat in his office, staring out of the window and writing down disjointed thoughts on scraps of paper. These he thrusts into his pocket, where eventually they become compressed into little balls.

Once, years before Dr. Reefy appears in the story, he was married. Again, on appearance, this was an odd, but nonetheless beautiful union. The girl he married had come to him because she was pregnant. But the father of the child was a man she did not love and did not wish to marry. Dr. Reefy had quickly grasped her circumstances. He greeted her with the words, "I will take you driving into the country with me." From that moment she knew that she never wanted to leave him. The two married and lived happily. He was able to discuss freely with her his ideas and dreams. She died after a year of marriage. Dr. Reefy was then left alone to think and write down fragments of ideas.

It is important to note, however, that unlike many of the other Winesburg grotesques, Dr. Reefy has never attempted to monopolize any concept or "truth" for selfish reasons. The happiest period of his life was that in which he enjoyed free and open communication with his wife—not when he was imposing his delusions upon someone else.

The comments made by the narrator about Dr. Reefy are important for understanding Anderson's attitude toward the majority of the grotesques in the stories. Dr. Reefy's marriage is characterized as "delicious, like the twisted little apples that grow in the orchards of Winesburg." Then the narrator explains that after the choice apples have been picked and sent to the cities "where they will be eaten in apartments that are filled with books, magazines, furniture and people," only the gnarled, twisted fruit remains. These are the sweetest apples of all, though "only the few know the sweetness of the twisted apples."

The twisted apples are a key image in *Winesburg*. Dr. Reefy's knuckles are described as resembling the misshapen fruit, and Anderson was later to refer to the *Winesburg* stories themselves in the same way. To him, the source of beauty lay in the nature of one's character. Though physically unattractive, Dr. Reefy possesses an inner beauty, which is reflected in his relationship with his wife. And in "Death," one of the later stories, he offers comfort to Elizabeth, George Willard's mother. He has an intuitive understanding of the problems of both women and offers unbounded sympathy.

To the citizens of Winesburg, Dr. Reefy is an eccentric outcast. In Winesburg, as in modern America, a man's conformity to establishd standards of appearance and behavior were of major importance. In expressing his own sympathy for Dr. Reefy and the other "beautiful" grotesques, Anderson is emphasizing to his readers that the means to understanding among human beings is through an appreciation of character. People who have been rejected by society for failure to conform to arbitrary social norms must be accepted on the basis of their feelings and motives. In this way, the walls that separate modern Americans can be breached.

Victims

A group of the *Winesburg* stories features characters whose lives have become misshapen through means other than self-assertion. They have become victims of the warped ideas of the unattractive grotesques— either acting individually, as a group, or even as an entire segment of society.

A good example is Wing Biddlebaum in the story "Hands." He is by nature intense. While he talks, his hands stay in perpetual motion, as if they were wings. As a young man, he was headmaster of a boys' school in Pennsylvania. There, he enjoyed talking for hours on end with his students,

. . . lost in a dream. Here and there went his hands,
caressing the shoulders of the boys, playing about the
tousled heads. As he talked his voice became soft and
musical. There was a caress in that also. In a way the voice
and the hands, the stroking of the shoulders and the
touching of the hair were a part of the schoolmaster's effort
to carry a dream into the young minds.

One youth he touched in this fashion was a half-
witted boy who formed a romantic attachment to his
teacher. He had fantasies of love between himself
and Wing and began talking with others about them.
Parents of the students became concerned and ques-
tioned their children about the teacher's touch. Immediately they assumed that he was a homosexual.
They beat him, threatened to lynch him, and drove
him from the town. He came to Winesburg, where
for twenty years he has employed his nervous hands
picking berries on nearby farms.

When Wing sees George Willard, he recognizes
him as a sensitive boy who should be encouraged.
One day, he attempts a serious conversation with
the boy. For a moment he lapses into the role and
mannerisms of his former schoolmaster self. His hands
begin to play about him. Suddenly, a look of horror
comes over Wing's face. He thrusts his hands into
his pockets; tears come into the eyes, and he walks
nervously away.

The trembling old man may be seen as a grotesque
—someone unable to talk naturally to others and
avoided by his fellow citizens of Winesburg. However,
Wing is portrayed as a thoroughly good and wholesome human being, who touches people out of love
and concern. He is a lonely person who craves closeness with others. The real grotesques in the story are
the parents in the Pennsylvania town, who act upon
an unfounded assumption, and the citizens of Wines-

burg, who ridicule his strange mannerisms. In ruth-
lessly imposing their mistaken perception of the truth,
they have made an innocent man an unfortunate
victim.

Elmer Cowley, in "Queer," has for years suffered
silently because he thinks of his family as being mis-
fits in Winesburg. His father, Ebenezer, has sold his
farm and bought a general store. Ebenezer has been
a miserable failure as a merchant, partly because he
feels ill at ease talking with people. His ignorance of
merchandising prompts him to purchase stock that
no one will buy. He allows the store to become filthy.
Generally uncommunicative, his favorite expression
is, "Well I'll be washed and ironed and dried!" Elmer
thinks that Ebenezer's unusual expressions, his unattractive store, and his awkwardness with his customers, cause people to see the whole family as queer.
He is therefore intent upon changing this image.

George Willard figures prominently in this story,
as a foil to Elmer. As a successful newspaper reporter,
George can express himself well. The townspeople
think he has a promising future as a writer. Elmer
strongly resents George's attributes, and one day he
expresses this feeling with desperate force. Early in the
day, Elmer has run a traveling salesman out of his
father's store by waving an empty pistol about and
telling him that he will do no more purchasing until
some sales are made, and that he wants no more queer
merchandise. But as he reflects upon his actions his
feeling of queerness increases. Several hours later, he
calls George Willard out of the newspaper office,
thinking in some vague way that discussing his feelings
with George may ease them. Elmer is unable to articulate any of his confused thoughts. When he tries to
talk, his arms move involuntarily and his face twitches.
He asks George to leave him.

He then returns to the store, takes twenty dollars from the cashbox, and prepares to run away on the next train. Just before the train leaves, he summons George to the train station. He is again unsuccessful in unburdening himself. All he can say is "I'll be washed," his father's expression that he hates so much. Then, he stuffs the bills he has taken into George's hands, admitting that he has stolen them. Unable to say anything more, he strikes out desperately with his fists and begins pounding George. As the train pulls out of Winesburg, he says to himself, "I guess I showed him. I ain't so queer. I guess I showed him I ain't so queer."

Elmer has arrived at this unhappy point by having been subjected to conditions over which he had no control. The father's eccentricities have made him ashamed, and his need to correct matters has turned into frustration. Again, it can be said that he is one of those Winesburg citizens whose miserable plight is imposed upon him and is not at all the result of anything he has consciously done or willed.

Dreamers

A few *Winesburg* characters possess the strength necessary to live happy, well-adjusted lives; all of these have a sense of hope. This is often expressed in the form of a dream, or ideal, toward which the character aspires. This possibility does not mean that the individual has escaped traumatic experiences; no one ever does. It does mean that despite whatever menacing circumstances are endured, these people show resiliency as well as the motivation to press forward.

The most obvious example of a dreamer is George Willard, the protagonist in "Departure," the final story. In a village that contains so many whose frustrations have made them inarticulate, his is an important role. Often, the grotesques and their victims come to George and attempt to unburden themselves, as if he were a father confessor, able to offer them salvation and release.

In the course of these encounters, George is drawn into their problems and actions. Yet, he is never adversely affected by these involvements. Neither is he threatened by his garrulous father Tom Willard or by the death of his mother, to whom he has been close. George leaves Winesburg when he is eighteen. Significantly, he sits on a departing train in a dream-like state and, in the closing words of the book,

. . . When he aroused himself and again looked out of the car window the town of Winesburg had disappeared and his life there had become but a background on which to paint the dreams of his manhood.

The fact that George is able to place the experiences of his years in Winesburg in the background of his mind should not be taken to mean that he was insensitive to them, or that he failed to perceive the significance of what he has experienced. It is rather a sign that his often painful experiences have not destroyed his capacity to dream, and it is his dreams that will provide direction and motivation in his manhood.

One of the characters George leaves behind in Winesburg is a little girl named Tandy Hard, who appears in "Tandy." She is the daughter of the town agnostic, who argues constantly against the existence of God. The little girl was named Tandy by an alcoholic who had come to Winesburg hoping to stop drinking. He had become a drunkard because he was "a lover and [had] not found his thing to love." In his suffering, he has come to recognize something sympathetic between himself and the child, who is only seven. He admonished her simply, "Be Tandy" which, he explained, "is the quality of being strong to be loved." At the end of the story, the little girl tearfully states, "I want to be Tandy . . . I want to be Tandy Hard."

Though she does not appear again in the stories, it seems safe to assume that by being able to imagine a condition that is pleasant and uplifting, the little girl may grow into a happy, normal adult. She has been given, in effect, a dream to pursue, and this dream may prevent her from becoming a grotesque or a victim.

It is, however, wrong to assume that all dreamers find happiness, for there is another type of Winesburg dreamer whose dreams are sometimes destroyed. Anderson implies that such people can become grotesques. At least this was the case with Wing Biddlebaum, for Anderson states explicitly that as Wing's nervous hands tousled the hair of the boys in his school he was attempting "to carry a dream into the young minds." Wing's capacity to dream, and in turn to convey dreams to others, was permanently destroyed by the cruel accusations of the parents of his students.

Elizabeth Willard, George's mother, is the classic example of the ruined dreamer. Her dreams have always been specific: she had wished to become an actress and to enjoy the stimulations of life in the theater. Elizabeth, however, was more willful than prudent, and she unwisely married the garrulous Tom Willard "because he was at hand and wanted to marry at the time when the determination to marry came to her." She has spent years chastizing herself for the unwise decision. Her health has failed, and at forty-one she appears much older than she actually is.

Elizabeth had paid frequent visits to Dr. Reefy, more for his patient understanding than for medical help. "Something inside them meant the same thing, wanted the same release." Both are dreamers who stand no hope of gaining fulfillment. One afternoon, she tells the doctor of her lost dream and of her unhappy marriage. As she speaks, she suddenly becomes animated, and her tired voice becomes clear and excited. Both doctor and patient sense the significance of the moment and they start to embrace. Just then a wooden crate is thrown onto the floor outside the office; Elizabeth becomes embarrassed and leaves. The intrusion symbolizes the destruction of the beautiful by the mundane in Elizabeth's life. She and Dr. Reefy never share such an intimate moment again. Perhaps both sense that a moment of that kind is spontaneous and that its memory would be spoiled by a self-conscious attempt at duplication.

As with many other Anderson characters, their lives are unlived in the fullest sense of the word. Both Reefy and Elizabeth may be grotesques in that they seize upon treasured dreams and hold on to them throughout their lives. But Elizabeth's dream of a theatrical career and Reefy's desire to find someone like his wife, who will give him sympathy and understanding, are beautiful, innocent dreams. Both of these dreamers are basically unselfish, loving, and intent upon close communion with mankind. It is in a sense tragic that the innocent dreams of deserving dreamers often go unrealized. But in *Winesburg, Ohio* dreamers such as Reefy and Elizabeth seem fated, either by external circumstances or by the nature of their temperaments, to dream in vain.

Anderson seems to be saying that every man is entitled to his dreams of self-fulfillment. Providing that these dreams do not jeopardize the happiness and well-being of others, they are to be nurtured and pursued. When one's pursuit is thwarted, whether by the actions of another individual or by external conditions over which he has no control, one is to be viewed as a pathetic grotesque, but not necessarily as unattractive. Despite her sickly appearance, Elizabeth remains beautiful throughout her life. Anderson uses the observations of both George and Dr. Reefy as a reflection of her loveliness. Both speak of her as "the dear . . . the lovely dear."

Winesburg, Ohio contains, on balance, more unhappy and unattractive grotesques and victims than optimistic dreamers. Anderson stated that collectively the tales formed "the story of repression, of the strange and almost universal insanity of society." Many readers have thought, therefore, that by showing the unattractive side of a large number of *Winesburg* characters, Anderson was attempting to denounce the small town and American culture in general. This is not actually so. His purpose was not to condemn American political systems and social institutions. He realized that most Americans were repressed without realizing it. He felt that if Americans could be made to see the extent of their repression in compassionate but unvarnished terms, individuals might be made more aware of the sufferings of their fellow beings and act with more understanding toward them.

At this early stage of his career, Anderson was without the specific suggestions for effecting closeness among people that he later envisioned. In *Winesburg*, he simply implied that people can become happy and complete when they possess the freedom to follow dreams and ideals, and that they should be encouraged, rather than thwarted, in this pursuit.

Anderson portrayed his fictional small town as being no better and no worse than any other part of America. He did not, as some have maintained, denounce village life. Indeed he felt angry toward Sinclair Lewis for depicting the town in *Main Street* (1920) as dull, physically ugly, and inhabited by ignorant, provincial people. Yet, Anderson cannot be characterized as merely an apologist for small towns. His is rather a balanced view, reflecting a mixture of praise and censure, both of the town and of the over-all civilization it mirrors.

Because it focuses upon a rural village, *Winesburg, Ohio* has been classified as one more installment in the tradition of American small-town literature.[2] Beginning with E. W. Howe's *Story of a Country Town* (1883) and continuing through Sinclair Lewis's *Main Street* (1920) numerous volumes of poetry, stories, and novels treated small American towns, sometimes praising, sometimes denouncing the quality of village life. Because Anderson was identi-fied with the midwest and had been born in a small town, and because it has been established that many people and landmarks from his native Clyde were in-corporated in the fictional Winesburg, some scholars have held that Anderson was simply following a ·trend of contemporary American literature.

Viewing *Winesburg* as merely another study of village life amounts to flagrant underestimation. The critic who spoke of the book as *Winesburg, Any-where*[3] states the actual scope. *Winesburg* should be seen as a microcosm of modern America and of the western world in general. Its citizens follow the same drives, are victimized by the same corrupting forces, pursue the same dreams, and enjoy the same pleasures as others of their generation, no matter where they lived. By portraying the contemporary generation in terms of the grotesques, Anderson provided a con-venient metaphor from which to view and judge his age.

In personal terms, it was a heroic statement. Dur-ing the unhappy months that he had been living alone in downtown Chicago and working in an advertising office, he had thought much about his boyhood and his family. He also thought about the thousands of nameless strangers he had seen in Chicago, and about his fellow tenants in the rooming house. These people were also lonely, lost in a confusing, impersonal society and too weak and broken to find happiness. Expressing the many people he contemplated in terms of grotesques represents a feat of artistic creation. It reflects the power of Anderson's subconscious mind to gather material from many sources and to synthesize it into a crystallized concept. It is particularly notable that he did so during a period of personal loneliness, despair, and uncertainty.

Like the group of Chicago artists with whom Anderson had associated, he was an experimentalist. The "genteel tradition"[4] of the nineteenth century, perhaps best exemplified by William Dean Howells, had held that subjects such as sex and psychological aberrations should not be expressed in literature, that only the "smiling"[5] aspects of life should be treated. To the Chicago artists, such conventions seemed arbitrary. Many features of American life offered nothing to smile about, and sex was a vital part of living.

Although he had no conscious desire to be shocking in his work, Anderson did feel the need to express himself frankly and honestly about controversial subjects such as sex and the frustration and desperation that seethed below the surface of American life. When *Winesburg, Ohio* appeared in 1919, this candor brought forth charges that he was shocking and immoral and even caused his work to be banned from a number of libraries. But to the American intelligentsia he was a pioneer who dared to say what others had feared to say in an honest, forthright manner.

Again like the Chicago group, Anderson experimented with form. In prose fiction, the carefully manipulated plots of nineteenth-century writers fell into disfavor. They were replaced by stories and novels that did not rely upon the progression of incidents toward a dramatic ending. In the short story, Anderson was the most notable innovator of the Chicago group. No attempt at summarizing the plot of an Anderson short story is ever completely successful, for he was not concerned with arranging events in an even progression. A human life lacked a defined pattern; it was comprised of many loose and disconnected elements. When he expressed this sense of formlessness in his short stories, he at first offended editors. Even Floyd Dell, a close friend and editor of the progressive magazine *Masses*, is said to have felt that some of the *Winesburg* stories were formless.[6] After publishing two, the magazine stopped accepting them.

Anderson, however, strongly defended the structure of the stories. Like many of his contemporaries, he understood that the form of literature can mirror the loose form of life and thus enhance its meaning. If life is not neatly plotted, then the absence of a neat plot in a story or novel could help convey this perception. This was what he meant when he observed that "With the publication of *Winesburg* I felt I had really begun to write out of the repressed, muddled life about me."[7] He saw life as being composed of powerfully dramatic and meaningful moments, but the structure of the *Winesburg* stories suggests that these moments occur infrequently, and not necessarily as the result of a logical progression of events. *Winesburg* characters are constantly doing surprising and bizarre things. The only way the writer can understand what prompts them is to probe into their troubled minds, where little sense of order or logic exists.

For instance, on the evening that Alice Hindman in "Adventure" runs naked through the streets, one would expect that the chain of events that culminates in such an act could be traced. But such a sequence is not to be seen in the story. Her day, spent clerking in a store, is not unlike the days of the last eleven years. It may be observed that a sense of lonely desperation weighs quite heavily, or that the rain depresses her, but she has experienced both conditions many times before. Anderson is making the point that her irrational behavior is a symptom of the "almost universal insanity of society,"[8] and that insanity is the very antithesis of logical order.

Anderson realized that in treating America within the Winesburg microcosm he was doing something innovative and vital in art. This is reflected not only in his own statements concerning the book, but in the guise and language of the narrator. It is known that during the composition of *Winesburg* Anderson was reading the Old Testament. Though he was not religious in the sense of affiliating himself with any established denomination, he appreciated the language of the Old Testament writers as conveyed in the King James Bible. Its influence, found in phrases and expressions sprinkled throughout the book, is to be seen most strongly in "The Book of the Grotesque." Here, in beginning his description of grotesqueness with the words "In the beginning when the world was young there were a great many thoughts but no such thing as a truth," the narrator sounds like the writer of Genesis.

Anderson had several reasons for adopting this voice. The simple, stately language of the King James Bible was well known to most American readers. Also, by echoing the Old Testament writers, Anderson gave the impression of wise old age. He was speaking, in other words, like an ancient sage. The tone of old age is maintained in all the stories. It seems appropriate to the narrator, who is omniscient; in the process of presenting the various stories, he furnishes information about the characters and their situations and offers frequent comments.

For instance, in "Hands," the narrator interrupts his account of Wing Biddlebaum's career as a teacher to declare that Wing was "meant by nature to be a teacher of youth." He also reminds the reader that Wing's temperament and talent were rare gifts, though often misunderstood. At the end of the story, he compares the swift fingers of the old man to a devotee saying his rosary. Such remarks are never gratuitous moralizings; they enrich the reader's understanding of theme and character. The result of such passages is increased confidence in the understanding and sensitivity of the narrator. His is more than mere omniscience; it is omniscience combined with a sympathetic feeling for the characters as individuals.

There is yet another possible reason for Anderson's adopting the persona of age and wisdom. In it, one can see reflected much of *Winesburg*'s historical significance. Anderson's friend Ben Hecht once remarked that Anderson had "re-invented the American soul."[9] It is in *Winesburg, Ohio* that the originality of Anderson's achievements can best be perceived. Realizing that he had developed an innovative structure for the short story, and that his idea of grotesqueness and his method of concentrating upon the troubled inner terrain of character was also new, Anderson obviously needed an appropriate style and language. By allowing his style to show the influences of the book that contains the classic statement of the creation of the world, he gave the impression of being the creator of a new order himself.

That this was a reason for using scriptural resonances is further borne out by the titles of *Winesburg* stories. All of the titles, most of them single words, state a generality. Some—"Mother," "The Philosopher," "The Thinker," "The Teacher"—suggest a category of person. Others—"Godliness," "Adventure," "Loneliness," "Drink," "Death," "Sophistication,"

"Departure"—are abstractions. These titles suggest stories of timelessness and universality—stories that pertain to types of people and conditions of people in all ages and in all places.

Anderson was offering fresh concrete examples as illustrations of these generalities. A story titled "Adventure," if found in a popular magazine, might suggest to the reader a series of thrilling and daring exploits of the sort associated with an adolescent series, such as Tom Swift or The Rover Boys. But to see adventure exemplified by a frustrated girl, whose pathological sense of loneliness prompts her to run naked through the streets, is to encounter it in an entirely new and unprecedented light.

One aspect of *Winesburg* that has made it popular to a broad spectrum of readers is the simplicity of its style. Anderson himself admitted the necessity for simplicity when he stated:

> . . . My own vocabulary was small. I had no Latin and no Greek, no French. When I wanted to arrive at anything like delicate shades of meaning in my writing I had to do it with my own very limited vocabulary.
> . . . There was the language of the factories and warehouses where I had worked, of laborers' rooming houses, the saloons, the farms.
> It is my own language, limited as it is. I will have to learn to work with it.[10]

In stating that his language was that of "streets," "factories and warehouses," Anderson was not referring to slang or to the idioms peculiar to any locality, trade, or social unit. He was speaking of plain Anglo-Saxon words chosen by Americans for everyday conversation. Slang and distinctive idioms suggest the peculiarities of a place or of an ethnic group; Anderson developed a style that cannot be placed in any such narrow category.

He took simple words and combined them in an

effective way that was peculiar only to himself. He defined this technique as follows:

There was a kind of poetry I was seeking in my prose, word to be laid against word in just a certain way, a kind of word color, a march of words and sentences, the color to be squeezed out of simple words, simple sentence construction. . . .[11]

Anderson's sentences, in *Winesburg* and elsewhere, are often loosely constructed, allowing for quick shifts and turns of thought. Though typical examples abound, the passage in "Paper Pills," in which Dr. Reefy's wife is described, serves well as an illustration:

The death of her [Mrs. Reefy's] father and mother and the rich acres of land that had come down to her had set a train of suitors on her heels. For two years she saw suitors almost every evening. Except two they were all alike.

The first sentence travels swiftly from the death of parents, to the girl's legacy, to her pursuit by "suitors" (a typical contemporary word, though less idiomatic than "boyfriend" or "beau"). The third sentence, "Except two they were all alike," is an example of Anderson's frequent use of elliptical construction.

For several reasons, it was essential that Anderson employ a technique that contained poetic elements. First, details bored him. By means of a poetic mode he could suggest a substantial amount of background using a few quick images. Second, poetry allows more freedom in the positioning of words. Third, poetry suggests the poet's emotional involvement with his subject. Therefore, when Anderson states that Dr. Reefy's story is "delicious, like the twisted little apples that grow in the orchards of Winesburg," he is sharing with the reader a personal savor of the subject.

The core of Anderson's poetic style lies in the suggestive, implicit nature of its language. Anderson intended that his narratives create general impressions.

This approach is exemplified in the story "Sophistication," in which he attempts to explain the process
of evolving from adolescence into adulthood:

There is a time in the life of every boy when he for the
first time takes the backward view of life. Perhaps that is
the moment when he crosses the line into manhood. . . .
Ghosts of old things creep into his consciousness; the
voices outside of himself whisper a message concerning the
limitations of life. From being quite sure of himself and
his future he becomes not at all sure. If he be an imaginative boy a door is torn open and for the first time he looks
out upon the world, seeing, as though they marched in
procession before him, the countless figures of men who
before his time have come out of nothingness into the world,
lived their lives and again disappeared into nothingness.
The sadness of sophistication has come to the boy. . . .

Though all words in the passage are easily understood, they frequently combine to form ideas that are
anything but simple and clearly realized. Notice such
expressions as "backward view of life," "line into manhood," "ghosts of old things," "voices outside himself," "limitations of life." Also notice such ideas as
the forgotten men of the past marching "in procession"
and of the coming of "the sadness of sophistication."
In deceptively simple words, Anderson is speaking of
sweeping ideas and concepts.

Consider, for example, the full meaning of cross-
ing the "line into manhood." With a half-dozen words,
Anderson has set up a resonant process within the
mind of the reader—one requiring that he visualize in
specific terms the range of meanings implied in a
simple and rather general expression. Perhaps the expression may recall to the reader the arrival of puberty
or the assumption of more responsibilities than were
borne in childhood. In any case, such ambiguous statements call for a high degree of reader participation in
the form of personal interpretation.

From the earliest appearance of the stories, readers have found the experience of discovering *Winesburg, Ohio* both revealing and moving. Although *Winesburg* called forth the anger of prudish readers and reviewers whose tastes had been shaped by the genteel tradition, to its defenders—who appreciated its frankness and honesty, who understood its innovations in style and form, and who enjoyed sharing Anderson's emotional bond of sympathy with the characters—it represented a momentous event in American letters. Anderson lived to see the objections of the moralists overshadowed by an ever growing number of defenders.

Between the appearance of *Winesburg* in 1919 and Anderson's death in 1941, American literature became increasingly frank in both language and subject matter. Numerous young writers—among whom were Ernest Hemingway and William Faulkner—carried on many of the innovations in the short story that Anderson had introduced. Toward the end of his life, Anderson proudly stated that in the brief space in which "a new born babe is growing to voting age" the *Winesburg* stories might "almost [have been] published in the *Ladies' Home Journal.*"[12]

3

Expressing the Inexpressible

"*The Dumb Man,*" the introductory sketch of the story collection *The Triumph of the Egg* (1921), shows Anderson in the process of writing a short story. He is contemplating five characters. Intuitively, he senses that within the group there is a significant story to be told. Four of the characters live together in a house—a young dandy who laughs continually; a worried old man with a white beard; a nervous man with wicked eyes; and a woman yearning to be loved. A fifth character—a white, silent man—comes to the house and goes to see the woman, though no interaction takes place between them, or between any of the other characters, for that matter. Anderson never succeeds in grasping the story adumbrated by the group. The entire sketch is narrated in Anderson's own voice rather than that of an assumed fictional persona. In the characteristic forthrightness of this voice, he freely admits, "I cannot tell it.—I have no words." He considers himself a "dumb man" for not being able to extract a story from his raw materials.

The point of the sketch is to describe the workings of Anderson's creative processes. It was his habit to select a person or situation that intuition told him was promising material for a story. He was quick to form an emotional bond with his subjects. Once the sympathetic rapport was established, he let his imagination pore over the subject, in the expectation that the significance of the situation would be perceived and that a story would flow. It was a method that revealed a need to love and feel close to people and things— a sort of passion to merge with them in understanding.

In "The Dumb Man" he explores his characters individually and collectively. He tries to understand the old man with the beard and the younger man with the wicked eyes, but he cannot. He speculates that the white, silent man who visits the woman may be death, and that the waiting female may be life, but he does not pursue this possibility. He is most strongly attracted to the dandy, who laughs incessantly. Anderson believes that if his imagination can only penetrate this character deeply enough, he may grasp the story that he feels is inherent in the cast of characters. He is unsuccessful.

The perceptive reader recognizes the laughter of the dandy as symbolic—an indication that life in its formlessness defiantly mocks the artist who attempts to create from it structure and order. The sketch can be taken as Anderson's implicit statement that life has no clearly defined pattern, except what man attempts to create out of his own imagination.

One of the few concepts shared by Anderson and literary naturalists, such as Stephen Crane and Theodore Dreiser, is the belief that life is not divinely ordered. This did not mean that he shared their pessimistic conclusion that existence is an absurd experience in which human striving comes to nothing. Rather, Anderson saw the meaning of life in the form of sympathy and understanding among people, and he felt obligated as an artist to bring this about. His characters are often the frustrated, the repressed, the weak, and the broken. But if he is able to understand them through the use of intuitive imagination, and in turn to articulate what he learns, he will have established a sympathetic bond among reader, character, and himself.

"The Dumb Man" ends with the simple statement, "I have a wonderful story to tell but know no way to tell it." Anderson seems to accept the fact that on this, and presumably on many other occasions, his creative processes have failed to perceive a story that would produce the kind of sympathetic bond he wanted to create.

In the "Foreword" to *Horses and Men* (1923) he faces a similar unyielding subject, as he sits at a table and contemplates an apple. It is a typical Anderson situation in that he senses that the apple possesses a hidden quality that has never been recognized or stated. Again, in the personal narrative voice of Sherwood Anderson, he muses that if, by means of intuitive imagination, he can perceive this quality and express it, man will be offered an element of sympathetic understanding with an everyday object that he may never before have recognized. Anderson again fails, and this time he voices concern over being unable to produce a story. He ends on a sadly plaintive note: "With these nervous and uncertain hands may I really feel for the form of things in the darkness?"

The reader tends not to see these two sketches as aborted stories. One is left with a feeling of sympathy for Anderson's honest, forthright attempts to capture the subtle and elusive qualities of life. All thoughtful people search for meanings they fail to find. The artist who honestly tries and fails is more their sympathetic partner than is the writer who has never dared to explore the depths of reality and who settles for presenting superficial details.

Anderson's fiction contains a minimum of detail describing the outward appearance of people, places, and things. Often, there is little indication of a particular time and place in his stories. His stories reveal

an impatience to get the surface details out of the
way so that he can get quickly to the essence of his
subjects. He was exceptionally adept at selecting one
or two details that immediately give the impression of
the entire subject. Of the appearances of the four men
in the room in "The Dumb Man," we know little. Yet,
on the basis of knowing only that one has a long white
beard, that one is dandified and laughs incessantly,
and that one has wicked eyes and moves about nervously, we have a distinct mental image of each.

Once Anderson was talking with Paul Rosenfeld,
the New York editor and critic, about policemen, for
whom Rosenfeld held considerable contempt. Rosenfeld could see nothing interesting or sympathetic in
the subject. But Anderson casually observed, "I see
them when they reach home at night. I see them taking
off their boots. Their feet hurt them."[1] Rosenfeld's
reaction to Anderson's statement is noteworthy, for it
describes the response of the average reader of Anderson's fiction:

Involuntarily my mind's eye met a small interior hovering
apparently at a short distance. It was the tenement kitchen
of some policeman in Chicago: what however filled the
cubicle was no battering-ram in blue but a coatless breath-
ing male in the suddenly significant act of taking off a
heavy shoe. An air of authenticity enveloped the picture.
The man's hand began kneading the foot uncovered in its
cotton sock. Instantly the interior turned into the unveiled
privacy of all policemen. Within the figure the nature of
men in general seemed rising to the surface. Promptly I
recognized a human being who got his bread with his
brawn and paid for it like everyone, with tired members.[2]

Rosenfeld's comments reflect Anderson's ability
both to suggest a large picture by means of a single
suggestive detail and his success in eliciting a sympathetic response from his audience—in this case one
who had expressed antagonism for the subject.

For Rosenfeld, Anderson's observation offered an extraordinary revelation: "No quite similar experience had ever befallen me," he admitted. "Through the image of a familiar, well-nigh grotesque, hitherto never clearly focused detail, I quickly saw an idea had been communicated to me; and at my own center, opposite it, antipathy and fear which hurt and shrunk me had been dispelled, and a confidence in life permitted to emerge, breathe, stretch itself."[3]

Anderson's observation on the policemen also shows that he approached his characters from the interior of their beings—from the standpoint of their feelings, emotions, thoughts—rather than from external appearance. This inner terrain shaped Anderson's sense of reality, which he readily admitted was difficult to define:

I do not know what reality is. I do not think any of us quite know how much our point of view and, in fact, all our touch with life, is influenced by our imaginations. . . . Having met some person for the first time . . . and having had my first look, I cannot ever see him or her again. . . .

Why is this true? It is true because the moment I meet you. . . my imagination begins to play. Perhaps I begin to make up stories about you.[4]

For Anderson, then, objective facts were less important than "facts" perceived through the imagination. One of his greatest strengths as a storyteller is the ability to perceive "imaginative" facts that offer unique insights into his subjects.

Frustration

That Anderson could find unique meaning in the most commonplace objects is obvious in "The Egg" (1920). Not only does a simple egg suggest to him a

bittersweet story of human frustration; it is also used
to symbolize the mysterious workings of nature. The
youthful narrator, one of several that Anderson employed in his early stories, is prompted by the events
of the story to ponder "why eggs had to be and why
from the egg came the hen who again laid the egg."

None of the three main characters—the boy and
his parents—is ever named. By making them anony-
mous, Anderson suggests the universality of their
plight. Until he was thirty-four, the father was a
farmhand. Then he married and was seized with "the
American passion for getting up in the world." The
means he chose for achieving success was chicken
farming. The boy was born during the first year of
this disastrous enterprise.

Throughout the story, the boy proves a highly
effective point of view. By speaking innocently of the
chickens' perilous struggle for survival and of his
parents' repeated failure to make money by raising
the delicate creatures, a powerful sense of dramatic
irony is achieved. A vast gap exists between the innocent relation of details and the far-reaching serious
implications that the boy is unaware of. The boy
speaks with candor and humor of fluffy chickens "such
as you will see pictured on Easter cards" becoming
"hideously naked." After eating quantities of food
"bought by the sweat of your father's brow," getting
diseases like the pip and cholera, "looking with stupid
eyes at the sun," the chickens die. To the boy, the
droll image of the naked bird looking stupidly at
the sun is humorous. But the reader sees reflected in
the picture a cruel nature that destroys the very
defenseless beings it creates.

After ten years of unsuccessful chicken farming,
the family moves to a nearby town in which the parents open a restaurant. But the poultry venture accompanies them in the form of several misshapen

chicks that have been preserved in bottles of alcohol. When the father places these freakish specimens on a shelf in his restaurant, an unsavory, bizarre element is introduced into the narrative. They symbolize the cruel workings of nature and foreshadow the futile attempt of a farmer to "get up in the world" by means of the restaurant business.

The farmer is an awkward, uncommunicative man. He has never dealt with the public and does not know how to attract trade to the restaurant. Finally he decides that he should try being jovial to his occasional customers and perhaps entertain them. The story comes to a poignant ending one rainy evening when the farmer tries to entertain a man at the lunch counter by showing him the deformed chicks in the bottles. When the shocked customer attempts to leave, the farmer detains him by proclaiming that he can fit an egg boiled in vinegar through the narrow mouth of a bottle. For more than a half hour he attempts this feat. Then, as his customer is preparing to leave, he pushes the softened shell too hard, and it breaks. The man leaves, laughing loudly.

The farmer, frustrated and angry, curses and hurls another egg after him. Then he gently picks up an egg and climbs the stairs to the family apartment. He gingerly places the egg on a bedside table and drops to his knees beside his wife, sobbing like a baby.

The farmer contains some elements of Anderson's father: he has grandiose ideas; his desire for success seems ill-starred; he brags of being able to do things he cannot accomplish. There can be no question about the boy's compassion for him, however. The boy freely admits that he is "the son of [his] father." Both boy and man stand awed and ineffectual before the paradoxical egg—so seemingly simple, yet so complex in defying man's attempts at understanding.

After seeing the father crying pathetically beside
his wife, the narrator admits at the end of the story
to "the complete and final triumph of the egg" over
the family's strivings. This admission represents a
change in the humor of the story. It now becomes a
kind of cosmic laughter—an attitude that suggests
laughter as an alternative to man's inability to understand the meaning of existence. Also suggested is the
cruelty that nature inflicts upon innocent creatures.
The father is as pitiable as the chickens. Both struggle
to survive in a world filled with obstacles. The odds
are against either succeeding.

"The New Englander" (1921) recalls the technique of the *Winesburg* stories in that its plot is developed by only a few incidents. Elsie Leander, an
unmarried woman in her mid-thirties who has grown
up on the family farm in Vermont, moves with her
mother and father to Iowa. She has lived a sheltered
existence with her parents. One day she watches her
niece and a farmhand embrace in a cornfield during
a storm and suddenly realizes that her protected life
has actually been one long episode of repression that
has thwarted her feminine impulses to love.

These details seem hardly sufficient for building
a story. Yet related by an omniscient point of view,
which focuses primarily upon Elsie's mind and emotions, they form a moving narrative. Elsie's native
New England is described with more detail than is
normally used in an Anderson story. Here it is done
in order to correlate character with setting. He speaks
of the New England landscape as containing "mangled
hillside[s]" and "gnarled orchard[s] surrounded by a
half-ruined stone fence." The Leanders are described
in terms suggesting thinness and paleness—lifeless
people shaped by worn-out soil and austere surroundings. By contrast, Iowa is a lush, expansive land, with

"fields that stretched away out of sight into the north, south, east and west" and land that is a rich black when plowed.

The Leanders have moved to Iowa in order to live near Elsie's brother. After being in Iowa for many years, the brother is robust and "inclined to corpulency," in contrast to his pale, white New England family. During the first planting season, a young Iowa farmer drives a six-horse team through a large cornfield while Mr. Leander works a tiny garden plot with a hand spade and his wife sits inside their house crocheting "little tidies."

Elsie's view of the new country is almost surrealistic, in that physical objects take on characteristics they do not actually possess. She sees the expansive newly plowed fields as a sea, and the family house as an island. The heaving breasts of the plow horses appear to her as giants' chests, which push the waters of the sea forward.

The subject of sex is never mentioned in the story; nevertheless the narrative bristles with sexual imagery. The warm, fertile earth that Elsie likes to touch is obviously a womb symbol. This is borne out by her seeing it in terms of a sea, which is recognized by some psychologists as a maternal symbol. The tall stalks of corn that spring from the warm black earth are obvious phallic symbols, and when Elsie becomes frightened by touching them, she is in reality showing fear and uncertainty concerning the opposite sex.

Elsie is only vaguely aware of the nature of her strange emotions; in her narrow, protected New England environment, she has never become aware of her sexual feelings. One Sunday, during the weekly visit of her brother's family, her strange new stirrings are especially strong. She knows that her niece has gone into the fecund cornfield to meet her lover. Elsie, who frequently stays away from the family dur-

ing her brother's visits, is standing behind the house
when she hears the beating wings of a bird trapped
in an abandoned room. Unconsciously, the sound of
the bird's wings makes her conscious of her own frustrated emotions, and of the strange feelings she has
experienced while standing in the cornfield.

Suddenly the bird escapes. Elsie instinctively flees
to the cornfield, in an attempt "to get out of her life
and into some new and sweeter life she felt must be
hidden away somewhere in the fields." As she runs,
her hair and clothes become disheveled. She continues
to move through the field as a storm rises, and she
hears her niece's name being shouted by the girl's
parents. Then Elsie comes upon the niece and her
lover, locked in an embrace. She drops to the ground
so as not to be seen. As her niece leaves to go to her
parents, Elsie remains on the ground as "something
within her was being twisted and whirled about as the
tops of the corn stalks were now being twisted and
whirled by the wind." As the torrents of rain begin
to fall, her internal storm "that had for years been
gathering," breaks. She sobs heavily.

Anderson notes, however, that her "storm of
grief . . . was only partially grief." This indicates,
apparently, that in expressing unbridled emotion for
the first time in her life—albeit an emotion of frustration and anguish—she has realized that she possesses a greater capacity for emotion than she has
ever suspected. The ending of the story skillfully
shows this. As her parents call her name, Elsie barely
hears their voices. The New England repression that
has fostered her frustration is becoming pale and
ineffectual now that she has experienced powerful
emotion for the first time.

"The Egg" and "The New Englander" imply that
the lives of average men and women are doomed to
frustration, both in attempting to understand and

control nature and in the achievement of emotional fulfillment. In these stories Anderson is suggesting that happiness lies in exploring nature to the fullest; in avoiding repression, if possible; and in allowing one's emotions to express themselves.

The Unlived Life

A frequent character type in Anderson's stories is the person who possesses a strong native capability that is never allowed to develop. In Anderson's view this is a waste, and he gives negative titles to two of his best-known stories containing such characters: "Unlighted Lamps" (1921) and "Unused" (1923).

Dr. Lester Cochran is a physician character who leads a solitary life, despite the fact that he comes into daily contact with the public. (This character appears in several stories.) A taciturn man, he develops strong and sensitive feelings for others that he is never able to express. Long before the story begins, he has treated an ill actress in a nearby town. After the girl recuperated, she married the doctor. They had one child, Mary. After Mary's birth, the doctor became increasingly less communicative, and the wife found that she could not continue to live with him. He understood this deficiency in himself and his wife's dissatisfaction, but he was unable to become more open. He took her to Chicago, where she could get a job with an acting troupe, thrust some money into her hand, and turned away without so much as saying goodbye.

He is as uncommunicative with his daughter as he had been with his wife. Mary is a basically happy, well-adjusted girl. But as she approaches maturity, she develops a strong concern over the lack of communication with her father, whom she loves.

The structure of "Unlighted Lamps" is typical of

Anderson's stories in telescoping details drawn from a broad expanse of time—in this case beginning at a point prior to the doctor's marriage. The central action, however, is concentrated within a brief span, so that the seemingly loosely related facts suddenly cohere in a short intense episode. The major action in "Unlighted Lamps" takes place in a single day. In the morning, Dr. Cochran tells Mary he has a heart condition that could cause his death at any minute. He relates these facts dispassionately and with characteristic awkwardness. In the brief hours that follow, Mary walks through the town and thinks about her father and about the way the family is regarded by the community. She knows that people think his taciturnity strange. She feels self-conscious, not knowing how she herself is regarded.

Mary's main concern is that her father's statement of his illness has not brought the two any closer. As she walks, she ponders the distance that lies between them. One of the people she encounters is a laborer, who recognizes her and tells her about Dr. Cochran's gifts of medical attention and money to his family. Mary wonders why a man can express kindly impulses in a material way while being apparently unable to express them directly. She remembers how as a child she has dreamed of the father's caresses she has never experienced.

During Mary's absence, Dr. Cochran is summoned to deliver a baby. The birth is a difficult one, and the doctor is exhausted after the labor is over. On his way back to the office he daydreams about his past. For over a year, he has often visualized the figure of a woman, whom he recognizes both as his wife and his daughter. He determines to try to breach the (to him) frightening gap between himself and his daughter. After returning his horse to the livery stable, he calls out "good night" to some men in the street in a voice so jovial that Mary is startled. As he starts up the stairs to the office, he falls backward, dead.

Anderson was predictably silent in fixing blame for the doctor's failure to communicate freely with other people. It is obvious, however, that he considers that the lamp of human affection has never been lighted within the doctor, and that this omission is a regrettable and tragic fact in anyone's life. Perhaps Anderson was implying that one never achieves a full sense of living by continually planning to do so; instead, one must live fully while one has the chance. Perhaps he was also suggesting that if the barrier to happiness was a trait such as reticence, it was up to the individual to attempt to overcome it.

"Unused" deals with May Edgley, one of Anderson's most completely developed characters. Early in the narrative May, the youngest girl in the Edgley family, commits an unprecedented act that surprises the town of Bidwell and sets into motion the course of events that leads to her death a short time later. May's two older sisters have become women of the street, causing the family to be shunned by the townspeople. May promises to be different. She is the most intelligent student in her high school and exhibits none of the attributes that have driven her sisters into their sordid lives.

In her seventeenth summer, May works as a picker on a berry farm, where she does her job silently and efficiently. One day, Jerome Hadley, a braggart from the town, joins the pickers, and May becomes talkative and even flirtatious. During the noon hour, while the other workers eat their lunch, May suddenly lays her food on the ground, climbs over a fence, and starts down a lane leading to a wood. After going a little way, she turns around and looks at Jerome, who immediately follows her. They do not return for two

hours. Later, he boasts to his cohorts that May was
an easy conquest.

This, the only sexual indiscretion in May's life,
causes the people in Bidwell to think that she has
the same wild blood as her sisters. The sisters themselves upbraid her for her action. Two recurring images are used in describing the reasons for May's lapse
and its aftermath. The first is the image of a stream,
which is used partially to explain her actions, partially
to suggest their ultimate results. After May first met
Jerome Hadley in the berry field, and became attracted to him, she allowed her imagination to fantasize
about being loved by a man. "She imagined arms
soft and yet firm, strong arms, holding her closely, and
sank into a dim, splendid world of emotion." Then
"the stream of life in which she had always wanted
to float had picked her up—it carried her along."

Because of the reputation of her sisters and the
indifference of her parents, May had never felt loved
or accepted despite her native intelligence and high
scholastic achievement. She has viewed the affairs of
life from the sidelines, never feeling that she was a
participant. She had read of but had not experienced
love, and had seen it debased by her sisters and disregarded by her parents. Her imprudent act with
Jerome Hadley represented an awkward, faltering attempt to enter the stream of life as a participant.

The second recurring image is a tower. It is first
mentioned just after a naive character named Maud
Welliver enters the story. May, sensing Maud's in-
genuousness, tells her that Jerome Hadley had followed her into the woods to ask her advice about a
love affair he was having with a married woman. May
says that Jerome had intended to kill the woman's
husband, but that she talked him out of it. She says
that he tried to seduce her, and, because she would
not submit, he spread the rumor that she had. This

lie, told in order to justify her act to herself and to convince Maud of her chastity, becomes "the first of the foundation stones" of "a tall tower on which she could stand, from the ramparts of which she could look down into a world created by herself, by her own mind."

From her fertile imagination, May creates a far-fetched tale of being courted by an Eastern prince, who is to return and marry her. Although Maud believes this story and comes to regard May as something of a romantic heroine, she invites her to a dance and arranges to have a grocery clerk escort her. In this final scene of the story, May is once again faced with a threatening situation reminiscent of the episode with Jerome Hadley. The dance is held in a seedy roadhouse. May, half believing the romantic fable she has told to Maud, feels quite superior to her escort. She wears her best clothes and a hat decorated with large ostrich plumes that was borrowed from her sister Lillian. As she listens in bored silence to the banal stories her escort tells, May watches the faces of the dancers. Suddenly she thinks of Jerome Hadley and is terrified that he may attend the dance. These thoughts weaken the tower of romance in which she has attempted to live for the past several weeks. She can no longer think of herself as a superior woman in boorish surroundings. She becomes simply a frightened girl trapped in a room full of raucous bumpkins that remind her of the rabble she has known all her life.

These memories mark the turning point in the story. They indicate May's descent to reality from the tower of fantasy that she has built in her imagination. In an attempt to escape from these past associations, she suggests to the grocer that they go outside; but as she rises, six ruffians from Bidwell arrive. One, Sid Gould, has been involved in a fracas over one

of May's sisters. When he sees May, he loudly announces that he intends to take her away from the
grocer. To quiet his boasting, May accompanies him
outside. But as soon as they are a little distance from
the roadhouse, she suddenly pulls away from him.
She grabs a piece of driftwood and begins swinging it
about, hitting Sid and knocking him down.

Then, beginning to run, she experiences a moment of self-awareness such as she has never known.
She begins to equate the incident with Gould with
her encounter with Jerome Hadley. She suddenly
realizes that the motive of both men has been not
merely sexual gratification but also a malign desire
to debase her. Although she had, in an innocent way,
given her body to Jerome Hadley, she retained her
inner sense of dignity and goodness. She has not made
any sort of moral compromise with her seducer; her
finest qualities of character remain "unused."

As May continues to run from Sid's boorish
friends, who pursue her a long distance, she is overcome by thoughts that the world contains people
who wish to destroy the character of others. Within
her erupts "a fear of life itself." She stumbles into a
stream which, like the stream of life she had sought
to enter by enticing Jerome Hadley, has a deceptively
strong current. She is swept away, but she seems in a
way happy—in being delivered from a hostile world,
secure in the realization of having been unused by
it.

When May's body is found a few days later, her
hand still clutches the plumed hat. As a symbol, the
hat has poignant meaning: it represents the life of
romance and gaiety of which she had dreamed, and
its whiteness suggests the purity she has retained. As
a heroine whose physical indiscretions have left her
character unsullied, May strongly resembles Gustave

Flaubert's Madame Bovary, a nineteenth-century literary heroine with whom Anderson was familiar. Like Emma Bovary, May has dreamed of rising from a base existence into a fulfilling life that offered love and excitement. When this is denied them, both women lose the will to live. Emma commits suicide; May willfully runs into a swift stream, obviously wishing for escape through death.

Unlike numerous Anderson characters who entertain vague dreams of beautiful and pleasant things, May Edgley possesses a high degree of intelligence. Given the opportunity to develop her mind and to pursue meaningful goals, she could have become a productive member of society and a fulfilled individual. Through no fault of her own, she was forced to live in a loveless, ignorant family and to associate with people who wished to take advantage of her innocence. The loss of the successful life that May could have lived is, in Anderson's view, a significant waste for which an uncaring fate can be blamed.

Initiation

Several of Anderson's early stories are narrated by an unnamed boy who follows the horse-racing circuit at midwestern county fairs, working as a swipe, or groom, for the horses. His world is bounded on one extreme by innocent horses and on the other by not-so-innocent human beings. Like the narrator of *Gulliver's Travels*, the boy often makes comparisons between horses and people in which the people appear inferior to the horses.

"I'm A Fool" (1922) contains a well-rounded characterization of the boy. His style of narration is unusual in Anderson's fiction in that it is informal

and larded with colorful midwestern idioms, somewhat reminiscent of *Huckleberry Finn*. "Gee whiz,
it was fun," he exclaims,

You got to a county seat town, maybe say on a Saturday
or Sunday, and the fair began the next Tuesday and lasted
until Friday afternoon. . . . It left you a lot of time to
hang around and listen to horse talk and see Burt [the
black trainer] knock some yap cold that got too gay, and
you'd find out all about horses and men and pick up a lot
of stuff you could use all the rest of your life, if you had
some sense and salted down what you heard and felt and
saw.

The passage is likewise rare in that its tone exhibits
enthusiasm and pleasure.

"I'm A Fool" concerns the conflict between
natural instinct and affectation. This is a subject
ideally suited for the ambiance of natural horses and
pretentious men. The conflict is centered in the boy,
who repeatedly expresses his dislike of pretense. Twice
he starts to tell about his grandfather, apparently a
prominent man in Wales, but each time he stops
himself, saying "never mind that."

He has left home at nineteen to follow the racing circuit because he loves horses and because he has
little patience with his family's concern for social
respectability. Before he leaves, his mother cries, thinking his job a disgrace to the family reputation, and
his ambitious sister protests loudly. Although he has
no patience with the attitude of his mother and sister,
he nevertheless admits that one should "put up a good
front." One Saturday, the day of a racing meet in
Sandusky, Ohio, he dons his best clothes—"my new
derby hat . . . and a stand-up collar"—and goes downtown to "[walk] with the dudes." He swaggers into
the largest hotel in Sandusky and orders three twenty-
five-cent cigars. When he enters the bar, he sees "a

fellow with a cane and a Windsor tie on, that it
made me sick to look at him."

"I like a man to be a man and dress up," the
boy observes, "but not to go put on that kind of
airs." The boy pushes the fop aside, "kind of rough,"
and orders a drink. Then, "just to show him something," he has another.

Thinking that sitting in a box seat is "putting
on too many airs," he buys the best seat in the grand-
stand. Soon, a well-dressed young man ushers his
sweetheart and his sister to a seat in front of him.
All three are about the age of the boy, and as they are
seated, his eyes meet those of the sister. Both blush,
and he is smitten. The party of three lose their first
bet, and the boy, seeing the horses taking positions
for the next race, taps the brother on the shoulder and
advises him how to bet. The brother asks him to join
the group. As he takes a seat beside the sister, Lucy
Wessen, he becomes conscious of his tipsiness and the
whiskey on his breath, and he blushes again.

As he joins the group, the boy evokes a genuine
pathos. Having disdained the customs and manners
of polite society, he feels a natural diffidence with
girls in general, especially one who obviously comes
from a privileged background. Still feeling the effects
of the whiskey, he is more unsure of himself than
he ordinarily would be. "Gee whiz, craps amighty," he
laments, "What a chump I was to go and get gay up
there in the West House bar, and just because the
dude was standing there with a cane and that kind of
necktie on, to go and get all balled up and drink
that whiskey, just to show off."

The boy realizes that the girl is sincere, genuine,
and can "talk proper grammar without being like a
school teacher or something like that." Nevertheless,
he tells "the smashingest lie you ever heard," about his
father being wealthy and owning a string of race

horses. Although he is careful not to do it "in no brag-
ging way," and only means "to start things and then
let them drag the rest out," he cannot restrain himself from trying to impress Lucy Wessen.

He and the brother bet on a horse he recommends,
and they win handsomely. They dine together and
take a launch to an amusement park, where they stay
until the Wessen trio leaves for home. The boy realizes
that Lucy "wasn't stuck on me because of the lie about
my father being rich and all that," but he is utterly
unable to admit to his lies. When they are alone, "I
most cried and I most swore and I most jumped up
and danced, I was so mad and happy and sad."

At the train station, she promises to write him
at the false address he has given her. When the train
leaves, he "busted out and cried like a kid." All he can
think of is the dandy with the Windsor tie at the bar.
Had it not been for him, the narrator would never
have drunk the whiskey and as a result told the elaborate lie that he is unable to rectify. The story ends
with the narrator angry both at the dandy and at himself:

I wish I had that fellow right here that had on a Windsor
tie and carried a cane. I'd smash him for fair. Gosh darn
his eyes. He's a big fool—that's what he is.
    And if I'm not another you just go find me one and
I'll quit working and be a bum and give him my job. I
don't care nothing for working, and earning money, and
saving it for no such boob as myself.

The boy's disgust with himself is natural. He has
been unaccustomed to drinking as much as he did, to
talking to the opposite sex, and to telling pretentious
lies. He has been cruelly initiated into the ways of
pretense and affectation, which have wounded his
simple, forthright sense of behavior. He calls the experience "a hard jolt . . . one of the most bitterest I

ever had to face." Even after considerable time has passed and he thinks of the incident, he wants "to cry or swear or kick myself."

Like the narrator of "I'm A Fool," Herman Dudley in "The Man Who Became A Woman" is an adolescent horse groom who experiences a cruel initiation. At nineteen Herman has "never been with a woman"; but he fantasizes about them by imagining how his ideal girl should look and "at night dreaming about . . . seeing women's bodies and women's lips and things. . . ." Too shy to talk to women, he often feels lonely and despondent, and finds the company of horses more congenial than that of men. He recognizes "how mean and low and all balled-up and twisted-up human beings can become . . . just because they are human beings and not simple and clear in their minds, and inside themselves, as animals are. . . ." The one being he shares a close rapport with is the horse Pick-it-boy; he says that each understands the other "in some way I can't explain."

One evening at the end of the racing season, when he feels particularly dejected and the image of his ideal woman is especially vivid, he has several drinks in a saloon. Then, peering into a mirror behind the bar, he sees "not [his] own face but the face of a scared young girl."

Although he admits that he has seen himself as a female on several occasions when he was "a young fellow" (the story is narrated at some point in adulthood, when he is happily married), he is stunned by the reflection in the glass. He hears laughter around him, and he imagines that the other men in the bar have seen the same feminine image. However, their laughter is directed at a strange-looking laborer with a crop of red hair that sticks straight up; he enters the bar with a little boy who looks just like him. The man orders a number of drinks in quick suc-

cession, muttering meaningless words under his breath
all the while. As he does this, a man in the bar
begins to imitate him, which brings gales of laughter
from the other drinkers. Suddenly the red-haired man
grabs Herman Dudley, shoves him against the bar,
and tells him to hold on to the little boy. Herman
watches as the red-haired man gives the teasing one a
sound beating, then grabs up his son and leaves.
Herman is left alone at the bar, unnerved both by
having seen himself as a woman and at almost having
been involved in the fracas.

Herman returns to Pick-it-boy's stall in a heavy
rain, half frightened, half dejected. He goes immediately to Pick-it-boy and begins "running my hands
over his body, just because I loved the feel of him and
as sometimes, to tell the plain truth, I've felt about
touching with my hands the body of a woman I've seen
and who I thought was lovely too." Calmed by his
closeness with the horse, he climbs to the loft above
the stall, removes his rain-drenched clothes, and
crawls, naked, beneath a stack of horse blankets.

Just after he falls asleep, he is awakened by two
black men, "half liquored up," who have seen him
climb into the loft and, at a distance, have mistaken
his young white body for that of a woman. He is
frightened both by the possibility of a homosexual
assault and by the fact that their mistaking him for
a girl reinforces his earlier fantasy of seeing himself
reflected as a female.

He frees himself from the men and, dropping to
the horse stall below, flees, still naked, into the rainy
night. He runs through a thick wood, bumping into
trees that bruise and scrape his body. Then he stumbles
and falls forward. Feeling himself entrapped, he finds
"white bones wrapped around [him] and white bones
in [his] hands." He has fallen squarely into the skeleton of a horse, lying near a slaughterhouse located

not far from the race track. "I seemed to find myself dead with blind terror," he later recalls, "It was a feeling like the finger of God running down your back and burning you clean. . . ."

The stumbling incident is actually a kind of bizarre initiation ritual. The white bones of the skeleton are stark symbols of death—a death of Herman's innocent fantasies of women and a death of his notions that the world of the race track is superior to the world outside. That the ambience of the race track can be cruel and uncaring is further emphasized when he returns to the track after the episode in the forest. He arrives just as daylight breaks and is greeted by the laughter and jeers of the other grooms.

He leaves as soon as he can get dressed. As his black friend Burt hurls curses at the laughing horsemen and defiantly shakes a pitch-fork at them, Herman is "cutting out along the fence through a gate and down the hill and out of the racehorse and tramp life."

Realization

From the mid-1920s onward, Anderson wrote short fiction only occasionally. Though he still sought within common objects for essences that often eluded him and still showed concern for unlived lives, debilitating frustrations, and the pains of growing up, many of the later stories state a marked affirmation of life and a profound respect for nature. "Death in the Woods" (1926) and "Brother Death" (1933), two stories from Anderson's final collection *Death in the Woods, and Other Stories* (1933), are forceful examples of these principles. In both stories Anderson employs the theme of death to emphasize the values of life and to express his respect for the workings of nature.

The central figure of "Death in the Woods" is
a bedraggled woman who in her youth worked as a
serving girl for a German family. The man she married has continued to treat her as a servant. Later,
so does her son. Both men see her merely as someone
to feed the mangy dogs they insist upon keeping. Her
entire role in life has been to feed—first the German
family, then her own family and the dogs. In accepting
the responsibility of feeding others, she has become
silent and resigned, her body stooped and her skin
wrinkled. Never rebelling at the lowly treatment she
has received from the Germans or from her own family,
she has suffered silently.

One snowy afternoon she walks to a nearby town,
where she barters eggs for some meager provisions.
A butcher takes pity on her and gives her a few bones
for the dogs that have followed her. On her way
home, she reaches a clearing in the forest through
which she has to walk and sits down beside a tree to
rest. She never rises. Perhaps tired from carrying her
load, perhaps too passive to leave the silence of the
clearing and resume her walk through the snow, she
falls asleep and freezes to death.

Just after she sat down, the dogs left her to chase
rabbits in the forest; it is a suggestion that the dogs
possess both the primitive traits of their wolf ancestors and a domestic instinct. As they chase the
rabbits, following their native killer instinct, their
domestic senses tell them that the old woman is dying.
They return to protect her. When she dies, they drag
her body into the center of the clearing and run in a
circle around her, as if performing a dance cele-
brating death. They eat the food in the bag that had
been intended for them. They do not harm her body,
although they rip her dress down to the waist. When
she is found several days later, face down in the snow,
the hunter who discovers her thinks that she is a

young girl. Her flesh has become smooth and white from exposure to the pure cold, and she looks beautiful in death.

Anderson states that the story was based upon an incident he remembered from his childhood. The old woman had lived near the Anderson home and had frozen to death in some nearby woods. He and one of his brothers had been present when her body was recovered. When they arrived home after the incident, his brother attempted to relate what had happened. "I do not think he got the point," Anderson confesses, "He was too young and so was I." Anderson narrates the story in the persona of a mature, middle-aged story teller; but he is still not satisfied with his telling. Like many of the subjects treated in his stories, this one contains a mystery and a significance that is subtle, elusive. In the many years intervening between the incident and the writing of the story, the strange events in the forest became "like music heard from far off." And he recognizes that "the notes had to be picked up slowly one at a time."

At the end of his story he admits that he was "dissatisfied then and [has] been ever since," with his attempt at conveying the significance of what had actually taken place. Nevertheless, one may infer significant meanings from his presentation of this "simple story."

The ritualistic dance of the dogs around the woman, seemingly purified by death, seems to celebrate the justice of nature's processes. Here, death seems to be one of nature's beautiful events, especially as it is contrasted to the cruelty and meanness that the husband and son have shown the old woman. Death thus becomes a triumph of nature's scheme over the miserable failure that man has made of life.

In his early fiction, Anderson had shown nature

as mystifying man by the intricacy of even its most commonplace objects (as in "The Egg") or as cruelly failing to create individuals strong enough to cope with the pressures of everyday existence (as in "Unused"). "Death in the Woods," while not indicating that Anderson had arrived at a deeper understanding of nature, does show his profound respect for some of nature's workings. In claiming the life of the old woman, nature has asserted a wisdom and a process that demand man's respect.

Anderson maintained that "Brother Death," (1933), another story that centers ostensibly upon death, was his best. In it, he uses death as a means of evaluating the quality of life as it is lived by the John Greys, a farming family in southwestern Virginia. The story successfully answers the question posed by one of the children in the family: "Life, what is it worth? Is death the most terrible thing?"

As the story opens, Ted and Mary, the youngest of the three Grey children, are examining two huge stumps, left from chopping down a pair of giant oaks. The children, who have witnessed the cutting of the trees, innocently feel the stumps. Ted asks whether the trees had felt pain from the saw and whether the stumps had bled—as a man would bleed when one of his limbs was amputated.

The children's conversation points to the major action of the story, which concerns a tense drama within the family. The mother, whose aristocratic Grandfather Aspinwahl planted the trees many decades before, does not want to see them removed. To her they are a symbol of the past grandeur of her family, who have lost most of their wealth and lands. Her husband, John Grey, had decided to cut down the trees because the shade they cast impedes the lawn he is cultivating. As, in his rise to wealth, he has acquired most of the property the Aspinwahls once owned, he views the trees as monuments to a decadent family.

Ted has a serious heart condition that can cause death at any time. His parents and older brother have protected him to the point of preventing him from enjoying play. When he is stopped from playing, he becomes tense, trembles, and turns pale. One day, as he and Mary splash about in puddles during a rain, the mother reprimands them. Ted runs to the barn to escape her, but Mary stands her ground. Facing her mother, she says, "You should have more sense, Mother. . . . You mustn't do it any more. Don't you ever do it again." The mother, torn between her wish to rebuke Mary and her recognition that Mary is right, turns and silently walks into the house. After this confrontation, Mary and Ted are given freedom. Secure in "their own created world," they enjoy doing things that might be potentially injurious to Ted. They no longer fear reprisal from the older family members. Ted does die a couple of years after the puddle episode, but he dies peacefully, in his sleep.

The brother Don, oldest of the Grey children, bears a physical resemblance to Mr. Grey, with "the same lines about the jaws, the same eyes . . . the same curious lack of delicacy of thought and touch—the heaviness that plows through, gets things done." At sixty, John Grey looks forward to the day when Don will take over the large farm. But when Mr. Grey suddenly decides to chop down the trees, Don sides with his mother. The argument that develops between father and son becomes a contest of two strong wills. Don threatens to leave home. The father simply says, "All right. Go then." After the trees are cut down and Don leaves, the family lives in silent tension for several days. Then Don returns.

Mr. Grey's only comment is "It [the farm] will

be yours soon now. You can be boss then." Anderson
interprets the words to mean that one must assert
authority in order to retain authority, but that "something in you must die before you can possess and
command." In other words, only by feeling the hu-
miliation of having authority imposed upon you can
you ever effectively assert it yourself.

Anderson believes that the price Don has to pay
in order to be an effective authoritarian is entirely
too high, in terms of its damage to his ego and pride.
In fact, he sees Don as having had to endure a living
death. Ted, who dies in his sleep and does not live
to assume authority over others, as Don presumably
does, is far better off than his older brother. For "he
never had to make the surrender his brother had made
—to be sure of possessions, success, his time to command—would never have to face the more subtle
and terrible death that had come to his older brother."

The answer to the question—"Life, what is it
worth? Is death the most terrible thing?"—is that life
is worthwhile only when one is allowed to actualize
himself in his own way, to be free from restrictions
imposed by anyone else—whether individuals or society. Having been allowed to live free and untram-
meled, if only for a brief time, Ted dies fulfilled. His
death is in a sense beautiful, suggesting peace and
happiness.

In describing Mr. Grey's decision to chop down
the trees, Anderson uses a favorite metaphor: the
wall. John Grey's precipitous actions create a wall of
estrangement, with Mary and Ted on one side and
the rest of the family on the other. Throughout her
life, Mary realizes its existence. Anderson calls this
process of isolation "a driving destructive thing in
life, in all relationships between people." Don is in
effect trapped behind the wall because he possesses
the same drives of ambition and greed as his father.

Having had to endure an ignominious death while he is alive, it follows that for him physical death will be a bitter event because it will separate him from the material things for which he strove.

"Brother Death" is one of Anderson's most powerful statements concerning contemporary America. It denounces materialism not because objects are intrinsically destructive or harmful, but because in the pursuit of material things man turns from human values, such as understanding and concern for his fellow man. To Anderson, the end of material gain does not justify the means of dehumanization. He is saying that America must learn to respect human values if its material achievements are ever to be anything other than empty symbols of selfishness and ruthless avarice.

The persons victimized by the greedy are not the only ones to suffer. For the materialists themselves relinquish the freedom to live their own lives spontaneously, to live without the concern for protecting their possessions. As Mary and Ted inspect the tree stumps shortly before his death, Ted asserts over and over again that "Only men got their arms and legs cut off."

4

The Longer Form

Poor White (1921)

For the novel Poor White (1921), Anderson chose a
setting in the middle 1880s—roughly the same period
that is the ambience for *Winesburg, Ohio,* which was
published two years before. *Poor White* can be seen
as a companion volume to *Winesburg* in that it deals
with the transition in the midwest from agriculture
and handcrafts to mechanization. The possibility of
producing goods at a faster rate than had formerly
been possible offered the opportunity for quick wealth
and positions of power. The chance to acquire these
spoils encouraged aggressive drives of greed and selfishness among people; the result in both *Winesburg* and
Poor White was alienation.

The alteration occurring in the midwest is traced
in the development of Hugh McVey, a typical repre-
sentative of his region. Hugh is an authentic "poor
white," a member of a class that is lazy and indigent.
He is the son of John McVey, a former tanner who
has become an idler in the "little hole of a town" of
Mudcat Landing, Missouri. In the first half of the
novel, one gets the impression that Hugh is big,
clumsy, and very lazy. He sits on the bank of the
Mississippi, fishing and daydreaming, apparently following no direction in his life.

When Hugh is old enough to take a job, Sarah
Shepard, wife of the railroad stationmaster in Mudcat Landing, hires him. His association with Sarah
and her husband represents a kind of geographical
allegory. From New England, she has read in the
novels of Horatio Alger of honest young boys rising
from rags to riches. She firmly believes that if Hugh
follows the New England virtues of hard work and
thrift, he will become a successful man. Her plans
for him parallel the pattern of change that was start-
ing in the midwest as a whole. Eastern manufacturing
interests, intent primarily upon economic expansion,
were moving into the indolent, sprawling midwestern
United States. New kinds of material success through
the efficient operations of mechanized factories could
now be achieved.

Hugh works hard sweeping the station and doing
odd jobs after he falls under the influence of Sarah's
ever-present driving force. He does, however, occasionally lapse into "the odd detached kind of stupor
in which he had spent so large a part of his life."
Sarah also sees to it that he reads, and for the first
time in his life he develops an interest in books.

Sarah Shepard is the first person Hugh can talk
to comfortably. He has been accustomed to solitude
and to daydreaming, and his talks with her are for
him an introduction to verbal intercourse between two
people. When the Shepards leave Mudcat Landing,
Hugh is placed in charge of the railway station. Constantly fighting the tendency toward indolence that
had characterized his existence before he knew Sarah
Shepard, Hugh stays at the station for a year. In those
months he does his job efficiently and forces himself
to continue reading whenever he has the time. The
more he reads, the more he scorns his fellow poor
whites in Mudcat Landing, and the more he wants to
learn about life.

Just after his father is killed in a brawl, Hugh
decides to leave Mudcat Landing. The year is 1886,
and Hugh is twenty. He drifts eastward for three years,
spending short periods in various places and picking
up odd jobs. He finally settles in Bidwell, a northwestern Ohio town with two thousand, five hundred
inhabitants. Bidwell is on the threshold of change as
Hugh arrives. The agnostic Robert Ingersoll has lec-
tured there and has started the citizens debating the
divinity of Christ. And "the cry 'get on in the world,'
that ran all over America at that period . . . rang. in
the streets." Bidwell had been a community of farmers and craftsmen. The craftsmen are represented by
Joe Wainsworth, a harnessmaker who creates his products by hand and who refuses to repair machine-
made harnesses. "Learn your trade," he tells his apprentice. "The man who knows his trade is a man.
He can tell everyone to go to the devil."

Since leaving Mudcat Landing, Hugh has shown
interest in no particular vocation. His main desire is
to "penetrate the wall that shuts him off from humanity," or to learn how to interact freely with others.
He has no specific idea how this is to be accomplished.
The job he takes as telegrapher at the Bidwell railway station is more a source of livelihood than a
means of putting him in touch with humanity. Finding that the job leaves him a good deal of free time,
he enrolls in a correspondence course in mechanics.

One spring evening, as Hugh is taking one of
his frequent solitary walks, he passes by a field. There
he watches a farmer and his family toil on their
hands and knees setting out cabbage plants. The
moonlight falling upon the bent figures lends the
appearance of a primitive ritual being performed.
Hugh watches as the bodies of the farmer and his
family move with machinelike precision down the
rows. Gradually he gets the idea that he can invent

a plant-setting machine that will relieve the drudgery
connected with setting plants by hand. Though his
familiarity with mechanical engineering is still limited,
he sets to work to acquire the necessary knowledge.

As Hugh's invention begins to take shape, he is
approached by young Steve Hunter, who offers to
promote the manufacture of the machine by obtain-
ing backing from wealthy Bidwell citizens. Word of
the new enterprise spreads, and changes begin. Cheap
shacks, to be occupied by workmen at the factory, are
built. The livelihood of hand craftsmen like Joe
Wainsworth, the harnessmaker, is threatened, as
people begin to buy machine-made harnesses from
mail-order houses. Allie Mulberry, who carves ship
models purely for enjoyment, is hired to carve a pro-
totype of the new setting machine. Even religion is affected by the promise of the new industry, as one citizen is heard to pray for the success of Hugh McVey.

One of the backers Steve Hunter obtains for
the factory is Tom Butterworth, a wealthy farmer and
a ruthless materialist. He represents a marked contrast to his daughter, Clara. She, like Hugh McVey,
is a quiet, reticent individual who longs to communicate with people but does not know how. Tom
Butterworth sees his daughter as someone requiring
the time and attention that could be given to making
money. He has sent her to the state university in the
hope that she will marry and cease to be a burden
to him.

When Clara returns to Bidwell from the university, she is confronted by the many changes brought
about by Hugh's inventions. In addition to the plant
setter, he has developed a corn-picker and a device
for loading freight onto railroad cars. New people,
many of them speaking in strange accents, have moved
to Bidwell. Her father is now half-owner (with Steve

Hunter) of the new factory that manufactures Hugh's inventions, and his greed for money has increased.

She finds Hugh to be considerably different from her father. She appreciates his indifference to money, and his desire to follow the occupation of inventing machines because it fulfills his need to create. At the same time, she senses that, like herself, he is troubled by the desire to communicate with others.

Although Hugh is attracted to Clara, he thinks of her as a "lady," and above his social station. He mutters, "I ain't fitten for her." He assumes that she intends to marry Alfred Buckley, a stranger who has been in Bidwell a short time and who has business connections with Tom Butterworth. When Hugh learns of Buckley's arrest by federal authorities, he goes to Clara and announces awkwardly, "I came here to ask you to marry me. . . . I want you to be my wife. Will you do it?"

The scene is seemingly ridiculous. Although in his mid-twenties, Hugh has never found the courage even to talk to a girl. He has felt sexual desire vaguely, and has fantasized about loving women. But whenever the possibility of sexual gratification has presented itself, he has always withdrawn from the scene. On the one occasion that he and Clara have been alone, he has been too ill at ease to speak. But within the context of *Poor White*, so much of which is centered upon the tortured emotions of Hugh and Clara, Hugh's action is credible. Had Hugh not blurted out his forthright proposal, he might never have found another means of approaching her.

Likewise uncertain with others, Clara readily accepts. "If we're going to do it there's no use putting it off," she replies. The two drive in awed silence to the county seat. Initially, at least, the fact that they are married does little to ease their feelings of estrange-

ment. It is several days before the marriage is con-
summated, and then it is done at Clara's behest. This
weakens, without destroying, the wall of alienation
that has separated both Hugh and Clara throughout
their lives from communication with others. Anderson is saying that the wall cannot be demolished by
one single event, however momentous, within the life
of an alienated individual. Alienation increases with
time; time is required to lessen it.

Despite their moments of closeness, the wall between Hugh and Clara builds itself again. One con-
tributing factor is a sequence of unfortunate reper-
cussions produced by his inventions. A socialist has
moved to Bidwell and makes speeches to the factory
workers that demand open revolution against the
factory owners and the overthrow of the capitalist
system. Pushed to the breaking point by his assistant's
talk of machine-made harnesses and of the need to
charge higher prices for hand-made harnesses, Joe
Wainsworth sharpens a leather cutting tool to razor
keenness and decapitates the man. He then shoots
Steve Hunter, who, he believes, is partially responsible
for the decline of the craft tradition and the changed
way of life in Bidwell. Wainsworth is captured in
the country, and Clara, Hugh, and Tom Butterworth
drive him and his captors into Bidwell. On the way,
Wainsworth lunges at Hugh, sinking fingers and teeth
into his neck. "It wasn't me [who killed Joe Gibson,]"
he screams, "You did it."

The incident causes an important change in
Clara's feelings for Hugh. Disgusted by her father's
greed, she has partially resented the fact that Hugh
works for him. But when she sees her husband sav-
agely attacked, she begins to feel a maternal affection for him.

Hugh still feels awkward with Clara. This is increased by his sense of guilt over having been, in a

sense, the cause of the events leading to the harness-maker's demented rampage. Moreover, he is continually troubled by his father-in-law's insistence that he produce new inventions even if it means stealing the ideas of other inventors.

On one level, Hugh is somewhat fulfilled by having produced a number of useful machines and by marriage and fatherhood. But he has never succeeded in carrying out his basic goal "to penetrate the wall that shuts him off from humanity." One day, as he is returning to Bidwell from a business trip, he reflects upon his career as an inventor and concludes that on the whole it has been unsatisfying. Sometime before, Hugh had picked up some colored stones from a lake shore and had put them into his pocket. As he sits in the smoking car of the train, he studies the colors of the stones brought out by the sunlight. He thinks of the other people on the coach and considers all of them happier than he is. Then, "the light that had played over the stones in his hand began to play over his mind, and for a moment he became not an inventor but a poet." Suddenly he realizes what he truly wants and what will make him happy: "He wanted men and women and close association with men and women. . . ."

When he arrives home, Clara comes to greet him. Earlier in the evening she has felt her unborn infant kick for the first time and she wants to tell him. When she sees his weariness, her maternal instinct is aroused once more. Since his experience on the train, thoughts of his wife have replaced thoughts of inventing, and he talks freely and intimately with Clara for the first time. As they enter the house, the factory whistles of Bidwell blast forth. Their sound symbolizes Hugh's emotional release from the pressure of feeling that the most important thing in life was inventing machines that would bring wealth to him and to those connected with their manufacture. He now knows that people are more important than machines, and that by concentrating his attention upon them, instead of on creations of metal and wood, he has the chance of tearing down the wall that had separated him from the rest of mankind.

The ending of *Poor White* seems to indicate that it is possible for some alienated individuals to learn to communicate wtih others and to enjoy a satisfying intercourse with the world. But the process by which this transformation is accomplished is handled less than convincingly. In fact, the last fifty pages of *Poor White* are among the least satisfying in the book, and they indicate certain weaknesses in Anderson as a novelist.

Anderson is commonly recognized as a writer whose forte is shorter forms such as the short story, the essay, and the impressionistic sketch. His long narratives tend to be disjointed. They do, however, contain effective short sequences. He defended this structure by observing that life was "a loose, flowing thing,"[1] punctuated by meaningful moments of vividness. "There are no plot stories in life," he maintained. *Poor White*, despite its frequent digressive passages, comes closer to being a sustained, well-integrated narrative than any of Anderson's other novels.

However, the final fifty pages, which attempt to summarize the first four years of Hugh and Clara's marriage, mar the unity achieved earlier. Anderson seems to have added his final section as a kind of afterthought, for he offers important incidents that should have appeared in the chronological sequence established in earlier sections of the book. This means that important facts are deemphasized. It also means that their effect upon the major characters goes unregistered. For instance, only on the final page of the story do we learn that the McVeys have a little girl. Surely Anderson, in his role as omniscient narrator, should have commented upon the effect the child must certainly have had upon Hugh's reticence. As it is, the reader can only conclude that the effect was negligible, which is unlikely.

Equally unconvincing is the assertion, made in the final dozen pages, that a handful of colored stones could bring Hugh to the apocalyptic realization that it is contact with people, not machines, that offers a possible release from alienation. It would certainly be more credible if examples of Hugh's emergence from alienation to open communication could be shown. The reader has only the promise, symbolized by the brief conversation with Clara and the shrieking factory whistles of Bidwell, that Hugh has indeed crept forth from his alienation and has attained freedom of communication.

Nevertheless, the strengths of *Poor White* far outweigh these weaknesses. In *Poor White*, more than in any other novel, Anderson strives to give his protagonist a distinctive physical appearance and to provide physical details of the two locations that figure most prominently in the novel, Mudcat Landing, Missouri, and Bidwell, Ohio. The big, lazy boy who lies in the sun and fishes from the Mississippi riverbank calls to mind Huckleberry Finn in appearance and action. Mudcat Landing, with its shanties and town loafers, resembles the tiny river towns that Huckleberry Finn had known earlier in the nineteenth century. Both Hugh and Huckleberry are authentic products of their native locality who grew up to question the opinions and values held by the region.

The entire movement of the narrative is from indolence and vagueness to definiteness. Hugh McVey evolves from a slovenly daydreamer, with no fixed purpose in life, to a resourceful man whose mind is

trained to solve specific problems. In plotting this
evolution, Anderson also plots the movement of the
midwest from a relaxed land of small farmers and
tradesmen, to whom time means little, to a booming
industrial region, that sees time as a means of mass-
producing goods and making money.

It is possible that Anderson had read the *First
Principles* of British philosopher and sociologist Herbert Spencer before writing *Poor White*; for Hugh,
like the midwest, follows the classic evolutionary pattern outlined by Spencer:

Evolution is an integration of matter and the concomitant
dissipation of motion; during which the matter passes from
an indefinite, incoherent homogeneity to a definite, co-
herent heterogeneity. . . .[2]

Anderson saw in this process an inevitable viola-
tion of certain values that were important in the
older midwestern society. Craftsmen who had formerly
produced items that reflected the love and integrity
of the maker were shunted aside as less expensive,
mass-produced objects began to appear. The love
between neighbors, and even between parents and
children—both important components of village life—
diminished.

Anderson effectively dramatizes these changes.
The style of the novel frequently rises to the level
of poetry, which emphasizes the banality of the new
order in contrast to the sweetness of the old. The
following passage contains images of both the old and
the new orders, presented in the lyrical voice that
characterizes several parts of the novel:

In silence the cabbage fields slept beside the roads in Ohio.
Not yet had the motor cars come to tear along the roads,
their flashing lights—beautiful too, when seen by one afoot
on the roads on a summer night—had not yet made the
roads an extension of the cities. Akron, the terrible town,

had not yet begun to roll forth its countless millions of rubber hoops, filled each with its portion of God's air compressed and in prison at last like the farm hands who have gone to the cities. . . .

When Hugh decides to create a machine that will benefit the farm laborers who set cabbage plants by hand, he performs a strange ritual. He has never invented a machine before, so the only way that he can conceptualize its working parts is to fall upon his knees and simulate with his own arms and legs the movements that he envisions a machine should make. Hugh seems to be making supplication to a sort of machine god—imploring him to inspire the invention —a device that will conquer the land. This ritual is a sort of black mass, a supplication to a malign deity who brings destruction to those things that are natural and human.

In this novel the expression of love of one person for another, as well as its absence, is communicated in a variety of ways, and in many instances with frankness that earned for Anderson the charge that he was a shocking and indecent writer. For instance, before her marriage, Clara has felt love for only two people. One is Jim Priest, the aged overseer on her father's farm. Each has an intuitive sense of this mutual affection, and the old man shows far more concern for Clara's rearing than her father does. The other is Kate Chanceller, a manlike girl whom Clara meets at college. At first, Clara sees in Kate's friendship a desire, similar to her own, for companionship and mutual understanding. Then Clara senses a change in Kate, and she becomes "not unmindful of the fact that their friendship had been more than friendship. Kate loved to hold Clara's hand and wanted to kiss her. . . ."

Although Clara never allows the relationship to develop into an overt homosexual liaison, she continues to find her close friendship with Kate one of the most meaningful relationships she has known. Clara's relationship with Jim Priest and that with Kate Chanceller—both of them somewhat unusual— underscore the lack of love shown by Clara's father and suggest her need for achieving the same closeness in her marriage.

Kit Brandon (1936)

Kit Brandon (1936), Anderson's final novel, is set in the 1920s. The times are defined by the Prohibition era, and the automobile has become a permanent fixture in American life. In *Kit Brandon*, the automobile is central to the action, as Anderson's last heroine is famous as a driver for a rum-running syndicate.

Kit Brandon is the intelligent daughter of an irresponsible Appalachian moonshiner and his slovenly wife. Raised amidst poverty, filth, and hard work, she had few pleasures as a child. During her fourteenth summer, her father summons her to the creek in which he is bathing and tells her to take off her clothes. She complies, but as he begins to bathe her, she realizes that he is making a sexual overture. This incident is the "sudden snapping" of the thin cord that binds her to her family. She grabs her clothes and flees, never to return.

Following the course of many girls from the mountain towns of the south in the years following World War I, she goes to one of the new mill towns and gets a job in a cotton mill. She attempts to obtain some education by taking night courses and by reading books such as Theodore Dreiser's *Sister Carrie*. She moves on to a job in a shoe factory, and then becomes a clerk in a five-and-dime store.

Her development is reflected in several foils. Frank, a tubercular factory worker, is the first person to whom she ever feels close. Shortly before his death, Kit allows him to make love to her because he craves a feeling of closeness to another person. Agnes, another fellow worker, is an angry radical who harbors a bitter hatred of the wealthy. Though Kit can never bring herself to accept Agnes's convictions, she nevertheless learns from her much about the social and economic structure of the 1920s. One of her closest friends is a girl named Sarah, whose guiding principle is "life's a game." Sarah participates in liaisons with numerous men wealthy enough to improve her own lot.

One of the lessons Kit learns from Sarah is how to manipulate people. Kit first puts the principle into practice with Gordon Halsey. This son of Tom Halsey, a wealthy bootlegger, meets Kit while she is clerking in the five-and-dime store. He tries all sorts of enticements to win her sexual favors, but she will not succumb. She knows that he is rich and weak, and that she is persuasive enough to convince him to marry her.

While courting Gordon, Kit meets Tom Halsey, and both she and the older man recognize that they share many qualities. Both possess a large measure of native shrewdness; both are ruthless in achieving personal ends. Each respects the other for having these qualities, and each realizes that Gordon, by contrast, is weak and shallow.

Within a few months after their marriage, Kit and Gordon begin to drift apart. He begins to pursue women and stays away from her for extended periods. Tom becomes concerned. His fondest ambition is to have grandsons who will be known as gentlemen, and his son's deteriorating marriage poses a threat to this dream. He continues to supply Gordon and Kit with money, however, and Kit uses her portion to buy mink coats, expensive automobiles, and countless pairs of shoes.

When Kit discovers Tom's displeasure over her failure to bring forth a grandson, she goes to him and offers to become a rum-runner in his organization. Thus begins the fabled career of Kit Brandon. In the few years that she drives in liquor caravans, she builds a reputation that takes on legendary proportions. Once, when federal revenue agents are pursuing a convoy of Halsey cars, she pulls out of a side street, crashes into the side of the government vehicle, and talks her way out of the situation while the other cars in the convoy escape.

Kit is often accompanied on liquor runs by Alfred Weathersmythe, the young scion of an old Tidewater Virginia family. His grandfather had been a Confederate hero, and his father is a member of the state legislature. But Alfred considers his father a hypocrite and wishes to become independent of him. Sharing his grandfather's love of adventure, Alfred joins the Halsey gang.

Tom Halsey, sensing that the boy is confused, vulnerable, and hostile to his father, convinces him to murder one of the men in the liquor organization who has threatened to turn Tom in to the federal authorities. By giving the gruesome job of assassination to the young aristocrat, Halsey perhaps believes he is demeaning a class of people with whom he has unsuccessfully tried to associate. Or perhaps, in getting a boy to perform such a dastardly act, he is indirectly showing his resentment toward his own son. Kit, however, sees Halsey's act as wanton exploitation of a sweet, sensitive person she has come to respect and admire. After the shooting, Weathersmythe runs away, and she never hears from him again. Kit never forgives Tom Halsey.

The federal net begins to close in on the Halsey operation, and Tom sends for Kit. Before she goes to him, Gordon returns. She has not seen him in months, and he is beside himself with fright at what may happen to him and to his father's empire. Kit and Gordon go to Tom's farm. There, during an altercation between the Halsey gang and revenue agents, the terrified Gordon shoots and kills his father.

Kit escapes the federal agents at the farm, and for a long time she avoids capture. Her photograph is now to be seen on FBI-wanted posters. She ponders what to do with her life now that her career as rumrunner is over.

The final section of the novel shows Kit pondering her past and assessing what she has achieved in life and what she still seeks. The conclusions she reaches are aided by young Joel Hanaford, the son of a prosperous legislator and judge. Like Alfred Weathersmythe, Joel considers his father a hypocrite. Joel has been wounded in World War I, and his father has used his injury to court the war veteran vote. Also, Mr. Hanaford prosecutes the men who make illicit liquor, while enjoying their product himself.

Kit senses in Joel a "bitter resistance to life," and this realization increases her self-awareness. As she views the boy's bitterness toward his family, she recognizes that since she left her own family her life has been one long sustained attempt to improve her own station in life. She has laughed at the weakness of her husband, whom she has manipulated for his money. She has taken daredevil chances driving liquor cars in order to enhance Tom Halsey's opinion of her. The novel ends as Kit, for the first time in her life, is "carried out of herself and of her own problem [of evading the law] and into the life of another puzzled human. . . ."

When Joel first appears, one is given the impression that he functions as a *deus ex machina* (a character who suddenly enters at the end of an unresolved plot and brings events to a conclusion). He has not appeared previously in the narrative, and to have him presented unexpectedly suggests contrivance rather than a logical development in the plot. Joel, however, is really a foil to Kit. The two are featured together to illustrate Kit's capacity for compassion and unselfishness.

In responding to Joel's rebellion and confusion, Kit finally comes to recognize a worthwhile purpose for her life. She too has been confused and rebellious. Most of her talents and energies have been used to gain material success and the admiration of Tom Halsey; but once achieved, both goals have proved empty and unfulfilling. Being older and more experienced than Joel, she realizes that she may be able to prevent him from making the same mistakes she has made. By responding maternally, rather than romantically, toward Joel, Kit shows that she expects to gain nothing more than the satisfaction of having helped a fellow human being.

In *Kit Brandon,* Anderson is quite specific on the subject of humanistic versus mechanistic concerns. He recognizes that the machine is a permanent part of American society. From her work in factories, Kit "had got the feel of machinery down into her veins, into all of her body." When she becomes a driver of liquor cars she soon develops "a kind of personal feeling about the machine she drove. It seemed beautifully alive to her."

The machine, then, is not intrinsically evil. As long as man remains its master, he can use it to achieve meaningful ends. It is only when the machine is given a position of too much importance in human life—when people are made to serve machines —that human values are destroyed.

It is significant that Anderson selects a woman to illustrate the mastery of the machine by a human being. In 1931 he had published *Perhaps Women*, a collection of essays and sketches maintaining that American women had not relinquished themselves to the control of the machine as American men had done. Kit is an example of a woman whose sense of self-awareness and whose emotional capabilities expand even though she is forced into close contact with machines. Indeed, becoming a crack driver of automobiles is an important factor in her growth. Driving awakens latent qualities of daring and courage that she never before realized she possessed. The novel, then, is a successful attempt to portray the harmonious accommodation of the humanistic and the mechanistic; it shows that, kept in the proper proportions, both can thrive within the lives of modern Americans.

Anderson's relationship to Kit was different from that of the protagonists of his earlier novels. Those novels had featured characters based either upon himself as a young man or upon imagined persons. The plots dealt with experiences remembered from his own life and from the America of the late nineteenth century. More than a year before *Kit Brandon* was published, he had spent several weeks interviewing Mrs. Willie Carter Sharpe, a woman rum-runner from southwestern Virginia whose exploits had become legendary and who was soon to be tried in one of the largest moonshining trials ever held in Virginia. From these interviews and from news stories of the trial proceedings, which he methodically pasted into a scrapbook, Anderson wrote his last novel.

In the opening chapter, he constructs an unusual narrative framework. It is unique among his novels in that Anderson and Kit, both speaking in the first person, act as narrators. "Her story came to me in fragments," Anderson explains. "We were together for that purpose, that I might get her story. . . ." Much of the account is related by Kit herself, though it is Anderson who controls the narrative. He frequently interrupts her to interpret or to digress from a fact she has mentioned by commenting, exclaiming, or by following a chain of connection between her remarks and something from his own imagination or experience. Although he did not share the narrative role in any other work, he had previously digressed from his own narrative by following far-reaching chains of connection and by interpreting and commenting. The essential difference in the plotting of *Kit Brandon* is that Kit, who is based upon an actual woman, carries much of the narrative burden.

One of the strengths of Anderson's narrative experiment lies in the attractiveness of Kit herself. Her flamboyant life style, her innate sensitivity and honesty, her growth from a deprived urchin into a woman who finds through experience a meaningful set of values upon which to base her life—all these attributes make her interesting to the reader. Moreover, after having lived for a decade in southwestern Virginia, Anderson had developed an empathy for the Appalachian mountaineer and had come to appreciate the virtues of independence and fortitude that the Scotch-Irish ancestors of these people had brought to America from the British Isles in the eighteenth century.

Anderson used the southern Appalachian region in much the same way that he used the midwest in his early novels: as a microcosm of contemporary America. *Kit Brandon* is as much a story of America during the prohibition era as it is a chronicle of a mountain girl's development. The prohibition amendment had been passed at the urging of zealous puritanical groups such as the Anti-Saloon League, who thought that if the sale of liquor were outlawed, a kind of moral utopia would be created in America. Instead, further corruption developed. Before the amendment was finally repealed in 1933, illicit liquor traffic had become a new American industry. Liquor barons such as Tom Halsey used their illegal profits to buy the cooperation of legislators and law-enforcement officials. And, like the factory owners that had appeared in the midwest in the late nineteenth century, Tom Halsey would sacrifice anyone in his organization, in order to protect himself. He paid paltry amounts for liquor made at great risk by small distillers and boosted the price tremendously.

Kit is able to retain a sense of inner wholeness while being threatened by the same external forces that weaken her counterparts in Anderson's fiction. She is exposed to selfishness, yet she remains generous. She is exposed to the machine, yet she holds on to human values. She encounters lonely, confused people, yet she is able to realize a sense of purpose and meaning in her life.

Like May Edgley in the story "Unused," Kit has not allowed the physical act of love-making to debase her. Though she has had many lovers, she declares, "Not a one has ever touched me yet." She has kept in reserve her sense of personal dignity and integrity; her character has remained intact.

Yet, Anderson felt that retaining a sense of selfhood was not enough; one must also exercise concern for one's fellow man. Kit does this to a greater degree than any other character in Anderson's fiction. She shows compassion for the laborers in the factories; she gives understanding and support to Alfred Weathersmythe. The outcome of her relationship with Joel Hanaford is never told, but his plight causes her to realize the importance of placing the well-being of others before her own. The story ends with Kit's realization that the confused, troubled Hanaford is

the person "with whom she could make a real part-
nership in living." She can therefore be happy because
she can give freely of her own strength and experiences to someone who needs them. Within the context of Anderson's novels, she epitomizes the virtues of
selflessness and compassion; she may be seen as Anderson's ideal protagonist.

5

The Expanding Circle

Sherwood Anderson's Notebook (1926)

In Sherwood Anderson's Notebook (1926), the first of seven collections of nonfiction he published in the final years of his life, Anderson focuses upon several contemporary Americans, among them photographer Alfred Stieglitz and authors Gertrude Stein, Paul Rosenfeld, Ring Lardner, Sinclair Lewis, and William Faulkner. Most essays and sketches that form the *Notebook* show Anderson as an artist-critic, commenting upon people and events in contemporary America. He is concerned over the fact that America has rushed blindly ahead on a course of "progress" toward material success that has left a spiritual void. Her towns are ugly; her people have lost a sense of beauty. What she calls literature is not a creation of beauty, but a glib depiction of surface details of an unattractive civilization. There is a need in native literature for the "subjective impulse," which calls for the writer to search for beauty at the core of life.

These statements are explicit expressions of much that had been and would continue to be depicted in Anderson's fiction. As such, they constitute a sort of companion to the novels and stories. Various "Notes Out of A Man's Life" serve the additional function of showing something of the creative process at work.

Many are based upon impressions that seem at first
glance but passing occurrences of insignificant value.
Yet Anderson repeatedly unifies and associates them
with matters of larger import, so that the result is a
poignant statement that transforms the original incident.

One group of notes contains a collage of seemingly diverse commentaries on New Orleans, an
early-morning feeling of depression, popular writers,
a letter received from a lady novelist, and a concern
for clarity in his own work. Focusing upon his feeling
of depression in the early morning, he skillfully pulls
together the musings into a well-unified statement.
The depressed feeling leads him to believe that he is
getting old and is growing resentful of those who are
strong and young. He decides that he cannot work
that day. The ultimate point he makes is his inherent
love of work:

I want to work. It is my life. I want to gather together the
thousand impressions of life that have come to me. I want
to put meaning and music into prose. . . . I put on my
clothes and go away. I feel like weeping when the day
comes wherein I cannot work.

The technique employed in this and numerous
similar instances is a familiar one. It has been employed time and again in Anderson's short stories and
often in his novels, which for the most part are loosely
connected pieces of brief fiction. It is the tradition of
the midwestern storyteller, which digresses over seemingly unrelated materials that are finally pulled together. The novelist Evan S. Connell has remarked
that the structure of pieces narrated in this fashion
suggests a figure eight—a tortuous veering from an
initial idea and an ultimate return.[1]

Less familiar than the structure of the *Notebook*

pieces is the selection of subject matter. Between 1916 and 1926, Anderson had mainly written fiction. His chief source material had been his own experiences. Under the influence of his exceptionally active imagination, his characters and settings had become composites of various people and places he had known. Beginning with the *Notebook*, however, he began to address himself to specific people and situations. Though he still shared an emotional involvement with his subjects, he was nevertheless making an attempt to treat material that he did not derive from his imagination. He was, in effect, attempting to depict in his work contemporary America and not merely the inner concerns, fears, and dreams of Sherwood Anderson.

Still, Anderson's motives had not changed. He continued to be concerned with Americans' tendency to compete rather than to love each other. He continued to think that American lives were devoid of beauty and a sense of the spiritual.

In 1926, the same year that the *Notebook* appeared, Anderson became a permanent resident of southwestern Virginia, where he had spent the summer of 1925. Thus, instead of viewing American life from the perspective of large cities such as Chicago, New York, and New Orleans, where he had lived for more than a decade, his perspective now became a country estate and a town of some four thousand residents.

Hello Towns! (1929)

Late in 1927, Anderson bought the *Marion Democrat* and the *Smyth County News*. Initially, he served as principal writer for the papers. In 1929 he published *Hello Towns!*, a collection of news stories, feature articles, and editorials gleaned from his first year as a journalist. The selections form a sort of chronicle of town life for this period.

This collection also reveals another facet of Anderson's writing. In the articles he assumes guises that do not appear in the prose he had published in magazines and in subsequent volumes of nonfiction. For example, realizing that the newspapers performed the important function of providing the inhabitants with local news, he often assumes the impersonal voice of the writer of plain reportage. More often, however, he speaks in an informal voice—rather like one citizen chatting with another. The characteristic tone of this guise is personal, subjective, and sympathetic. Writing, for instance, of the arrest of a local moonshiner, he began his story thusly:

Sheriff Dillard has a notion that Ellis Cornett, who lives up Kentucky Hollow way, above Atkins, ought to see a doctor about his eyesight and smelling organs. The sheriff was up that way one day last week. They dug up two barrels of perfectly good mash in a barn just 147 steps from Ellis Cornett's door. . . .

And such a smell, the sheriff said. Mr. Cornett swore he did not know it was there.

The humor evident in this story—which Anderson captioned "Tough Luck in Turkeypen Hollow" —is also to be seen in the creation of several fictional characters who played a satirical role in his newspaper columns. The best known of these was Buck Fever, a young mountaineer who migrated across the hills from the mythical Coon Hollow to become an apprentice reporter on Editor Anderson's city newspaper. Buck commented on town events such as court cases, elections, and meetings of civic clubs. He frequently spoke of Marion inhabitants and criticized the stinginess of his boss, who never seemed to pay him enough. The pieces written in this persona make up Anderson's largest body of humorous writing.

Collectively, *Hello Towns!* reflects an extensive involvement in town life. It contains articles in which Anderson made appeals for contributions to the town band and fire department. He launched a campaign to clean up an unsightly dump. He advertised recently published books that readers might borrow from the free lending library he established in the newspaper office.

Anderson had bought the newspapers at a time of crisis, when he had serious doubts about his ability to produce additional fiction and, one may infer, growing misgivings about his marriage to Elizabeth Prall. Writing for the newspapers had kept his pen active with a kind of writing that was less demanding than fiction, but that nevertheless offered certain artistic opportunities, such as the chance to create the imaginary personas. Perhaps the major benefit, however, was that he came to recognize that nonfictional writing offered many creative possibilities, which he would exploit at length during the next decade.

Perhaps Women (1931)

Perhaps Women deals with the depression years.[2] The 1930s were ushered in by the virtual collapse of the American stock market in the autumn of 1929. The initial shock wave of economic troubles began on October 23, when the prices of stocks, many of which had been purchased on margin, began to fall sharply. Within three weeks, thirty billion dollars had been lost. The effects of the Wall Street debacle were felt in every segment of America's working population. But it would take years before the full extent of the disaster would be realized or before corrective measures could be effected. It is commonly agreed that 1932 was the bleakest year of the depression. Unemployment reached an estimated height of seventeen million. Wages had dropped off sixty percent from their 1929 level, and businesses lost between five and six billion dollars during 1932 alone. By 1933, 85,000 businesses had failed.

The gross income from American agriculture fell from its 1929 level of almost twelve billion dollars to only $5\frac{1}{4}$ billion in 1932; yet farm production declined by only six percent. In many parts of the midwest, farmers struck against the lowered farm prices. Many farmers in various sections of the country watched foreclosure auctions of their mortgaged lands and equipment.

Herbert Hoover, who was serving his final year as president in 1932, came to symbolize the governments' inability to deal successfully with the growing problems. In the spring of 1932, more than twenty thousand World War I veterans, who had been promised a bonus in their government benefits by the Patman bill in 1924, marched on Washington demanding immediate payment. Though the benefits were not due until 1945, Congress had overridden Hoover's veto and paid about half of the bonus. The ex-soldiers now demanded the other half. Their demands were met with tear gas and bayonets wielded, ironically, by American troops under the command of General Douglas MacArthur. Two veterans were killed by policemen, and numerous others were seriously injured.

By the end of 1932, during Hoover's last few weeks in office, confidence flagged in American banking. The demand for cash from certain banks was so great that numerous bank holidays were declared in order that panic might be averted. Before the end of 1932, more than six thousand banks had closed and nine million Americans had seen their savings disappear. On Hoover's final day in office, 13 March 1933, the American banking system had ceased to function.

Sherwood Anderson's primary concern during the depression was, predictably, the impact of the large economic and political forces on the people. Social historian Frederick Lewis Allen has observed that "the major phenomena of the depression were mostly negative and did not assail the eye." But he summarized a number of specific manifestations of the sort that attracted Anderson's concern:

First the breadlines in the poorer districts. Second, those bleak settlements ironically known as 'Hoovervilles' in the outskirts of the cities and on vacant lots—groups of makeshift shacks constructed out of packing boxes, scrap iron, anything that could be picked up free in a diligent combing of the city dumps: shacks in which men and sometimes whole families of evicted people were sleeping on automobile seats carried from auto-graveyards, warming themselves before fires of rubbish in grease drums. Third, the homeless people sleeping in doorways or on park benches, and going the rounds of restaurants for left-over half-eaten biscuits, piecrusts, anything to keep the fires of life burning. Fourth, the vastly increased number of thumbers on the highways, and particularly of freight-car transients on the railroads: a huge army of drifters ever on the move, searching half-aimlessly for a place where there might be a job.[3]

Perhaps Women is the first of four prose volumes that treat the depression years from the human point of view. Eleanor Copenhaver had inspired Anderson's interest in the working girl in southern factories, and he had accompanied her on numerous visits to both the girls and their employers. Anderson's focus in *Perhaps Women* is not, however, trained upon those problems that the depression had produced for the factory girls. He is rather concerned with an older problem: the machine and its erosion of human strengths.

The controlling idea of *Perhaps Women* is stated in the introduction: "Modern man is losing his ability to retain his manhood in the face of the modern way of utilizing the machine and . . . what hope there is for him lies in woman." Man has come to rely upon the machine to perform his labor and to create the products he uses. Working and creating are man's chief sources of strength, and by relinquishing them, man has become weak and even impotent. But women, according to Anderson, are most at home in the machine age:

It is a factual age, and in a factual age women always rule. In the world of fact every woman has the advantage of me because she has something I cannot have—the machine cannot touch her mystery—. . .

An important motif in *Perhaps Women* is Anderson's fascination with machines, especially the automobile. Seeing nothing inherently wrong with machines, he places blame for their dehumanizing influences upon what American people have allowed machines to do to their lives. Anderson's sustained cry is for human control over the monsters—the control that men have not exercised.

Several of the sketches deal with Anderson's tour of a southern factory, where he perceives, somewhat mystically, a bond between the factory girls and the spinners and looms, which they operate with feeling and mastery. His conclusion is that "if these machines are ever to be controlled, so that their power to hurt men, by making them impotent, is checked, women will have to do it."

No Swank (1934)

In *No Swank*, Anderson addresses what he perceives as a changing mood in America during the depression. Before the tragedy the country had prided itself on the accomplishments of many individuals who had distinguished themselves from the masses in various ways. Anderson maintained, however, that the strength of America was not found in powerful individuals— "our bankers, our big industrialists and the other, so-called American kings"—but rather in the democratic ideal of unity, brought about by all people working together toward common goals. One of the positive effects of the depression, he felt, was a decline in the individualism that had separated people and a growth of the democratic dynamic that unites them.

No Swank is a series of character sketches of a number of his friends who embody "no swank," or sense of self-importance, but who instead believe in working together within a democratic context. The writers Theodore Dreiser, Ring Lardner, and Gertrude Stein are included, as are the actor Jasper Deeter and the woodcut artist J. J. Lankes. But the focal personality of the collection, treated in the sketch "No Swank," is Henry Wallace, Secretary of Agriculture in the Roosevelt administration and a personal friend of Anderson.

Wallace had been a Democrat but four years when he led Roosevelt's presidential campaign in the midwest in 1932. After Roosevelt appointed him Secretary of Agriculture in 1933, one of his primary responsibilities was administering the Agricultural Adjustment Administration (AAA), which was designed both to raise the level of declining farm prices and to conserve the soil and supplies of farm products.

The AAA was one of the most active governmental agencies during the depression years, and Wallace proved to be an able leader. He was elected Vice President in 1940, and was named Secretary of Commerce in 1945.

Anderson, however, saw Wallace as a modest man who "doesn't talk too loudly" and who could be taken for a "farmer, college professor in some small Middlewestern college, country town storekeeper, country town postmaster." The final view of Wallace shows him just after an old farming friend, now one of his subordinates, has addressed him as "Mr. Secretary"; tears are running down his cheeks. To Anderson, the trend away from swank was a "humanizing" force in America—a movement toward achieving a heightened sense of civilization. "There is this desire among men, here in America just now, to like and understand each other. It is a pretty dominant hunger among us." Wallace and the other subjects in *No Swank* had, in Anderson's opinion, helped to facilitate this movement by personal example.

Puzzled America (1935)

Puzzled America (1935) is a collection of essays reiterating Anderson's hope for unity through true democracy. Written during the first six months of 1934, they are the result of Anderson's observations during an extended trip through parts of the south and midwest during the late winter and spring of that year. As usual, his primary interest on the expedition was the human story—an attempt to determine how the great depression was affecting the lives of individual Americans. His travels took him to the shacks of miners whose meager wages, paid in scrip, would not buy enough food at the company store to subsist on. He talked to unemployed tradesmen who had become beggars in order to survive; to workers striking for decent wages; to laborers on government relief programs.

Puzzled America contains Anderson's optimistic belief that solutions would be found for the problems of survival and unemployment. This belief was founded upon several bases. The first was Anderson's faith in the Roosevelt administration. In 1932 Franklin D. Roosevelt had campaigned upon a promise of "a new deal for the American people." By the time Anderson began the *Puzzled America* essays, Roosevelt had been in office for almost a year, and many of his recovery schemes were already implemented and were proving successful. Roosevelt was especially concerned about the American worker, whom he referred to as the "forgotten man."

Roosevelt had sponsored much legislation aimed at creating jobs for the unemployed. Anderson made frequent references to the effectiveness of such newly established programs as the NRA (National Recovery Act), TVA (Tennessee Valley Authority), and CCC (Civilian Conservation Corps). In "Blue Smoke," the tobacco farmers look to a government program that insures them reasonable prices from tobacco brokers and large tobacco companies, who have formerly attempted to keep prices low. In the CCC teams that are building roads in "Tough Babes in the Woods" and assisting archaeologists in "Mound Diggers," there is a healthy feeling of togetherness and of useful work being done. The CCC workers are not only enthusiastic about discoveries being made in the Indian mounds; they are pleased to have discovered jobs they would never have known about without the CCC program.

A second basis for Anderson's optimism was that he had sensed among the American people a willingness to support a plan that would relieve the various forms of suffering caused by the depression, even though the people as a whole did not yet agree about what that plan should be. Many believed that the great depression was occasioned by the collapse of the capitalistic system, which had allowed wealth to be distributed unequally and had thus created a society of a very rich minority and a very poor majority. Communist agitators visited the unemployed and promised an equal distribution of wealth under a Marxist government. Unionizers began moving south, demanding the right of collective bargaining for workers in factories, which factory owners admantly opposed. Others believed that the capitalistic system could be repaired, and that Roosevelt had the ability to insure both free enterprise for the factory owners and decent benefits for the workers. Each of these proposed plans seemed reasonable to portions of the population, but still the people as a whole remained puzzled as to which would be ideal.

Anderson recognized a third cause for optimism in the reserve of strength shown by the suffering American working man. "Elizabethton, Tennessee," a sketch treating one of the new industrial towns in his own region, ends with a description of a monument built of brick and thinly coated with concrete.

Already it was falling to pieces. How I would have liked to see one of those delicately featured, hard-boiled little mountain girls, done in stone by some real artist, standing up there on the main street of that town.

He recognized, moreover, the powerful weight of the labor vote. In "They Elected Him" and "Olsonville," Anderson discusses two dynamic politicians,

Senator Rush Holt of West Virginia and Governor Floyd Olson of Minnesota, who had recently been elected, largely by the working man. Anderson believed that both men were honest and worked hard to represent the needs and wishes of their constituencies; they were living manifestations of the principle that in a democracy government can be changed in accord with the requirements of the people.

The European noblewoman featured in "The Return of the Princess," the final selection, confirms Anderson's conviction that the American people retain a large measure of strength. Driven from her homeland during World War I, she came to America, stayed a few years, and returned to Europe just before the stock market crash in 1929. She has returned just after Roosevelt's election in 1932. She tells Anderson that in spite of the great depression she still sees in America something "that, compared to Europe, [is] gay and alive." "You do not yet have the fear," she says, the fear that pervaded totalitarian countries. America was still free to seek its own solutions.

To Anderson, the solution was already being manifested. He was convinced that democracy was the political system that was best for the country, and that Roosevelt was the leader who could make its benefits available to the people as a whole. "We are still at heart a democracy," he proclaims. "The hunger to do the thing together is still alive in us." In "At the Mouth of the Mine" he summarizes the hope he shares with his countrymen by paraphrasing a statement made by one of the miners:

If some one man can go through it—a Roosevelt or some other—if he can lead us into something new—the workers having a real chance—if he can do this without the terror or revolutions—it's worth a shot, isn't it? . . . Let's give this democracy thing another whirl yet.

Home Town (1940)

As the decade of the 1930s passed, and Anderson saw
the effects of the depression diminishing, he began to
express private fears over the rise of Nazism and
fascism in Europe. He was particularly disturbed by
the Nazi invasion of Poland in September, 1939, but
public events were not his major concern at this time.
Now in his mid-sixties, he realized that if the United
States became involved in European conflicts, a
younger generation would be the active participants.
He was enjoying his happy marriage to Eleanor, occasionally escorting her to professional assignments, and
viewing his own life and career retrospectively.

During the last two years of his life, he worked on
two projects that would constitute a summarizing
statement of his attitudes, arrived at after a quarter
century of exploring and writing about life in America. The first was *Home Town* (1940), a lengthy essay
accompanied by dozens of photographs of American
small towns taken by the Farm Security Administration.[4] Having begun life as a citizen of small midwestern towns, Anderson had traveled widely and
lived in large cities, and then returned once more to
a small town. *Home Town*, which centers upon a
composite town called "Oak Hill," recalls many details of American village life found in his early fiction
and reiterates much that was said and implied in
Hello Towns!

Recalling these experiences, he asks, "What's the
matter with Oak Hill?" "Why not Oak Hill?" These
are not mere rhetorical questions. The lengthy essay
and the dozens of photographs constituting *Home
Town* testify to the wholesomeness of life he had experienced in the Oak Hills of America. In the opening
pages of the essay, Anderson makes reference to the
important role that Springfield, Illinois, played in the

life of Abraham Lincoln. He maintains that it was because Lincoln learned to love and respect the "common folk he met in little country courtrooms" that he was able to protect the interests and well-being of every American.

In the nineteenth century, immigrants of many nationalities came to America and settled in small towns, where they learned the democratic ideal. And even though Anderson realized that the small-town experience was gradually disappearing because of industrial growth and the trend of many village people to move to cities, he continued to think that the democratic ideal was being developed in small communities, rather than in the large cities.

Like *Hello Towns!*, *Home Town* discusses the civic club, the church, the newspaper office, the courthouse and the changing seasons and their effect upon town life. Perhaps the most imaginative section of the essay is Chapter VIII, which describes numerous prototypes among the small-town citizenry. The village industrialist, the female hypochondriac, the town bully, the woman of mystery, again evidence Anderson's great talent at creating a vivid general picture by means of a few revealing details.

It is significant that Anderson wrote *Home Town* in his mid-sixties. Had he written such a book when he was younger, the result would surely have been different. Though he was certainly not the severe critic of small towns that he was often accused of being, the town as depicted in his fiction, and even in *Hello Towns!*, is pictured as comprising both wholesome and unpleasant characteristics. The sympathetic portrayal in *Home Town* reflects both the intervening experience of broad travel and city living and the mellowness of age, which often discards the unpleasant facets of one's youth and recalls only its happy aspects. Though Oak Hill may have its industrialists and bullies, it reflects the most pleasant qualities of small towns, remembered nostalgically by an aging writer. Indeed, it is "an elegy for a time and place that Anderson knows no longer exists [*sic*] and yet that he knows is part of his life."[5]

Sherwood Anderson's Memoirs (1942)

At his death, Anderson left some three thousand pages of an autobiography on which he had been working sporadically during the last two or three years of his life and from which he had published several excerpts. This largely unfinished work has been twice edited and published as *Sherwood Anderson's Memoirs*.[6] Consistent with his former treatment of reality, the *Memoirs* (1942) show the play of the artist's imagination over family, friends, and former experiences.

The structure is a series of essays that highlight individual facets of Anderson's life. Chronology is for the most part disregarded as he moves about in time, associating ideas, incidents, and people encountered at various periods. He was not attempting to compile a methodical factual record; he was seeking to interpret selected segments. Often the emphasis is placed upon other people—not necessarily the "notable" men and women with whom his reader would be familiar, but more often the "obscure" people "who have given [him] life." He restates the conviction, found in "Brother Death," *Kit Brandon*, and elsewhere, that the life of the fulfilled individual is not a thing apart to itself; rather "all lives merge." "When one writes of self one inevitably makes a hero of self. . . . I want to use my life only as a kind of springboard."

Anderson was still attempting to penetrate

through appearance to essence, but this time he was aiming at a final and enduring statement concerning his own life. While admitting periods of intense unhappiness and occasional defeat, he regarded his life as a full, rich experience. *A Story Teller's Story* (1924), had focused upon the formation of Anderson the artist. The *Memoirs* shows Anderson as the intense participant in life, which was, even in his mid-sixties, a continuing series of adventures, fully sensed and enjoyed.

Anderson admitted that his life contained "something of struggle," part of which involved having had to conquer a colossal ego. The interest and compassion he had shown for others represented a victory of sorts over this force. He had found peace and domestic happiness; he had seen his faith in the American people and in the Roosevelt administration rewarded by the gradual easing of the great depression. He focused upon the close bond among men, as exemplified in his many friendships, that he liked to think was manifesting itself in America.

The final section of the *Memoirs*, "The Fortunate One," serves to unify the variegated component essays by restating a theme that is used to introduce the volume: Anderson's gratitude for having been one of "the lucky ones" of his generation. Anderson despairs of the time in which he was writing (the late 1930s) which, he predicts, future generations will look upon as "another dark age." "Any civilization absorbed in economics, in war, in the economic interpretation of history, etc., can be but a savage and brutal civilization." He also admits that he has not always been successful in his writing and that he has often had to endure periods of "black gloom." On balance, however, "The Fortunate One," reflecting the entire contents of the *Memoirs*, is a sort of celebration of life as Anderson has known it. In this final summing-up, it is "the full rich life" he has lived, and not what he has written, for which he wishes to be remembered.

Having come from a family indifferent to a formal religion, he had never been a religious man in the sense of affiliating with any religious denomination or sect. He maintained that the meaning and ultimate goal of life was not an immortal life after death; rather whatever meaning life might contain was to be derived from the "great adventure" of earthly existence. Although he wrote that he accepted Christ, he quickly added that he thought that Christianity, as man has construed it, had become corrupt. For Anderson, Christ symbolized selfless love of others—a virtue that he, functioning with a secular context, had emphasized again and again in his work.

In the closing paragraph, he lists other aspects of life that he has found meaningful. "I have been healthy and strong . . . I enjoy my friends, women, food, drink, sleep. There is a kind of persistent youth in some men and I am one of that sort."

Notes

1. American Adventure

1. Howard Mumford Jones and Walter B. Rideout, eds., *The Letters of Sherwood Anderson*, p. 305.
2. Jones and Rideout, *Letters*, p. 305.
3. Jones and Rideout, *Letters*, p. 305.
4. Paul Rosenfeld, ed., *Sherwood Anderson's Memoirs*, p. 3.
5. Quoted in William A. Sutton, *The Road to Winesburg*, p. 517.
6. Francis Russell, *The Shadow of Blooming Grove: Warren G. Harding and His Times* (New York and Toronto: McGraw-Hill, 1968), p. 42n.
7. *A Story Teller's Story*, p. 7.
8. Rosenfeld, *Memoirs*, p. 118.
9. Sutton, *Road*, p. 181.
10. Sutton, *Road*, p. 236.
11. Sutton, *Road*, p. 238.
12. Jones and Rideout, *Letters*, p. 404.
13. Quoted in Sutton, *Road*, p. 247.
14. Jones and Rideout, *Letters*, p. 145.
15. Elizabeth Anderson and Gerald R. Kelly, *Miss Elizabeth: A Memoir*, p. 176.
16. "Nearer the Grass Roots," *The Outlook* 148 (1928), p. 4.
17. Anderson and Kelly, *Miss Elizabeth*, p. 189.
18. Jones and Rideout, *Letters*, p. 220.
19. One of the most succinct and informative treatments

of the causes and effects of the great depression is Milton Meltzer's *Brother, Can You Spare A Dime: The Great Depression, 1929–1933* (New York: Alfred A. Knopf, 1969), which supplements factual history with period songs and graphics. Broader treatments include Dixon Wecter's *The Age of the Great Depression, 1929–1941* (New York: Macmillan, 1948) and Frederick Lewis Allen's *Since Yesterday: The Nineteen Thirties in America, September 3, 1929–September 3, 1939* (New York: Harper & Brothers, 1939). A helpful collection of personal accounts and recollections of the period is Louis (Studs) Terkel's *Hard Times* (New York: Pantheon Books, 1970).

20. Held in Amsterdam August 27–29, 1932, the World's Congress against War attracted delegates from twenty-seven nations who were concerned about the rising threat of Italian fascism and German Nazism. But the moving forces behind the meeting were of leftist persuasion, and from the proceedings a document, *Manifest—War Congress Against The Imperialist War,* emerged, strongly denouncing capitalist politics and extolling the "systematic peace policy followed by the Soviet Union."

21. Rosenfeld, *Memoirs,* p. 3.

22. Rosenfeld, *Memoirs,* p. 3.

2.   RE-INVENTING THE AMERICAN SOUL

1. Parts I and II are both called "Godliness"; Part III, "Surrender"; Part IV, "Terror."

2. See, for example, Anthony C. Hilfer, *The Revolt from the Village, 1915–1930* (Chapel Hill: The University of North Carolina Press, 1969) and Ima Honaker Herron, *The Small Town in American Literature* (Durham, North Carolina: Duke University Press, 1939).

3. Sutton, *Road,* p. 441.

4. See especially Malcolm Cowley, *After the Genteel Tradition* (Gloucester, Massachusetts: P. Smith, 1936).

5. In *Criticism and Fiction* (New York: Harper & Brothers, 1891), Howells maintained that "the more smiling aspects of life" were "the more American."
6. Sutton, *Road*, p. 434.
7. Jones and Rideout, *Letters*, p. 93.
8. Jones and Rideout, *Letters*, p. 44.
9. Ben Hecht, "Go, Scholar Gypsy" in Paul P. Appel, ed., *Homage to Sherwood Anderson*, p. 149.
10. Rosenfeld, *Memoirs*, pp. 242–243.
11. Rosenfeld, *Memoirs*, p. 243.
12. Rosenfeld, *Memoirs*, p. 296.

3. Expressing the Inexpressible

1. Paul Rosenfeld, "The Man of Goodwill" in Paul P. Appel, ed., *Homage to Sherwood Anderson*, p. 4.
2. Rosenfeld, "Goodwill," p. 4.
3. Rosenfeld, "Goodwill," p. 4.
4. "A Writer's Conception of Realism" in Paul Rosenfeld, ed., *The Sherwood Anderson Reader*, p. 338.

4. The Longer Form

1. Quoted in James Schevill, *Sherwood Anderson: His Life and Work*, p. 96.
2. Herbert Spencer, *First Principles* (New York: D. Appleton, 1896), p. 396.

5. The Expanding Circle

1. Evan S. Connell, review of Ray Lewis White, ed., *Sherwood Anderson's Memoirs*, The New York *Times Book Review* 10 August 1969, p. 24.
2. The discussion of the early depression years that follows draws heavily from the opening chapters of both Frederick Lewis Allen, *Since Yesterday: The Nineteen Thirties in America* (1939) and Milton

Meltzer, *Brother, Can You Spare A Dime?: The Great Depression* (1969) (See above, Ch. I, n. 19).

3. Allen, *Since Yesterday*, p. 60.

4. The Farm Security Administration was established under the Resettlement Administration (a New Deal agency) in 1935 and was absorbed by the Department of Agriculture in 1937.

5. David D. Anderson, *Sherwood Anderson: An Introduction and Interpretation*, p. 155.

6. Paul Rosenfeld, ed., *Sherwood Anderson's Memoirs* (1942); Ray Lewis White, ed., *Sherwood Anderson's Memoirs* (1969).

Bibliography

1. Works by Sherwood Anderson

Fiction

Windy McPherson's Son. New York: John Lane Company, 1916; rev. ed., New York: B. W. Huebsch, Inc., 1919.

Marching Men. New York: John Lane Company, 1917.

Mid-American Chants. New York: John Lane Company, 1918.

Winesburg, Ohio. New York: B. W. Huebsch, Inc., 1919.

Poor White. New York: B. W. Huebsch, Inc., 1921.

The Triumph of the Egg. New York: B. W. Huebsch, Inc., 1921.

Many Marriages. New York: B. W. Huebsch, Inc., 1923.

Horses and Men. New York: B. W. Huebsch, Inc., 1923.

A Story Teller's Story. New York: B. W. Huebsch, 1924.

Dark Laughter. New York: Boni and Liveright, 1925.

Tar: A Midwest Childhood. New York: Boni and Liveright, 1926.

A New Testament. New York: Boni and Liveright, 1927.

Beyond Desire. New York: Liveright Publishing Corporation, 1932.

Death in the Woods. New York: Liveright Publishing Corporation, 1933.

Kit Brandon. New York: Charles Scribner's Sons, 1936.

Plays: Winesburg and Others. New York: Charles Scribner's Sons, 1937.

Nonfiction

Sherwood Anderson's Notebook. New York: Boni and
    Liveright, 1926.
Hello Towns! New York: Liveright Publishing Corporation,
    1929.
Perhaps Women. New York: Liveright Publishing Corpora-
    tion, 1931.
No Swank. Philadelphia: The Centaur Press, 1934.
Puzzled America. New York: Charles Scribner's Sons, 1935.
Home Town. New York: Alliance Book Corporation, 1940.
Sherwood Anderson's Memoirs, edited by Paul Rosenfeld.
    New York: Harcourt, Brace and Company, 1942.
Sherwood Anderson's Memoirs: A Critical Edition, edited
    by Ray Lewis White. Chapel Hill: The University of
    North Carolina Press, 1969.

Special Collections

The Sherwood Anderson Reader, edited by Paul Rosenfeld.
    New York: Houghton, Mifflin Company, 1947.
The Portable Sherwood Anderson, edited by Horace
    Gregory. New York: Viking Press, 1949.
The Letters of Sherwood Anderson, edited by Howard
    Mumford Jones and Walter B. Rideout. Boston: Little,
    Brown and Company, 1953.
The Buck Fever Papers, edited by Welford Dunaway
    Taylor. Charlottesville: The University Press of Vir-
    ginia, 1971.
*Sherwood Anderson/Gertrude Stein: Correspondence and
    Personal Essays,* edited by Ray Lewis White. Chapel
    Hill: The University of North Carolina Press, 1972.
The 'Writer's Book,' edited by Martha Mulroy Curry.
    Metuchen, New Jersey: The Scarecrow Press, 1975.

2. WORKS ABOUT SHERWOOD ANDERSON

Bibliography

Gozzi, Raymond D. "A Bibliography of Sherwood Anderson's Contributions to Periodicals." *The Newberry Library Bulletin* Second Series, No. 2. (1948): 71–82.

Rideout, Walter B. "Sherwood Anderson." In *Fifteen Modern American Authors: A Survey of Research and Criticism.* Durham, N.C., 1969, pp. 3–22.

Rogers, Douglas G. *Sherwood Anderson: A Selective, Annotated Bibliography.* Metuchen, New Jersey: The Scarecrow Press, 1976.

Sheehy, Eugene P. and Kenneth A. Lohf. *Sherwood Anderson: A Bibliography.* Los Gatos, Calif.: The Talisman Press, 1960.

White, Ray Lewis. "A Checklist of Sherwood Anderson Studies, 1959–1969." *The Newberry Library Bulletin* 6(1971): 288–302.

White, Ray Lewis. *Checklist of Sherwood Anderson.* Columbus, Ohio: Charles E. Merrill, 1969.

White, Ray Lewis. *Sherwood Anderson: A Reference Guide.* (In preparation.) Boston: G. K. Hall, 1977.

Essay Collections

Anderson, David D., ed., *Sherwood Anderson: Dimensions of His Literary Art.* East Lansing: Michigan State University Press, 1976.

Appel, Paul P. *Homage to Sherwood Anderson.* Mamaroneck, N.Y.: Paul P. Appel, 1970.

Asselineau, Roger, ed., *Configuration Critique de Sherwood Anderson, la revue des lettres modernes,* Nos. 75–80. Paris: M. J. Minard, 1963.

Campbell, Hilbert H. and Charles E. Modlin, eds., *Sherwood Anderson: Centennial Studies.* Troy, N.Y.: Whitston Publishing Company, 1976.

Rideout, Walter B., ed. *Sherwood Anderson: A Collection of Critical Essays.* Englewood Cliffs, N.J.: Prentice-Hall, Inc., 1974.

White, Ray Lewis, ed., *The Achievement of Sherwood Anderson*. Chapel Hill: The University of North Carolina Press, 1966.

Special Periodical Issues

The Newberry Library Bulletin Second Series, No. 2(1948). (Sherwood Anderson Memorial Number).

The Newberry Library Bulletin 6(1971). (Special Sherwood Anderson Number).

Shenandoah (The Washington and Lee University Review) 13(1962). (Sherwood Anderson Number).

Story 16 (September–October 1941). Reprinted in *Homage to Sherwood Anderson*, edited by Paul P. Appel (*q.v.*), pp. 1–160.

The Winesburg Eagle (Official publication of The Sherwood Anderson Society, The University of Richmond).

Biography and Criticism

Adams, Mildred. "A Small-town Editor Airs His Mind." *New York Times Magazine* (22 September 1929): 6, 20.

Anderson, David D. *Sherwood Anderson: An Introduction and Interpretation*. New York: Holt, Rinehart & Winston, Inc., 1967.

Anderson, Elizabeth, and Gerald R. Kelly. *Miss Elizabeth: A Memoir*. Boston: Little, Brown and Company, 1969.

Anderson, Karl. "My Brother, Sherwood Anderson." *Saturday Review of Literature* 31 (4 September 1948): 6–7, 26–7.

Blankenship, Russell. *American Literature as an Expression of the National Mind*. New York: Holt, Rinehart & Winston, 1935, pp. 665–72.

Burbank, Rex. *Sherwood Anderson*. New York: Twayne Publishers, 1964.

Cargill, Oscar. "The Primitives." In *Intellectual America*. New York: Macmillan, Inc., 1941.

Chase, Cleveland B. *Sherwood Anderson*. New York: Robert M. McBride Company, Inc., 1927.

Ciancio, Ralph. " 'The Sweetness of the Twisted Apples':
    Unity of Vision in *Winesburg, Ohio.*" *Publications of
    the Modern Language Association of America* 87 (Oc-
    tober 1972): 994–1006.
Cowley, Malcolm. "Anderson's Lost Days of Innocence."
    New Republic 142 (15 February 1960): 16–18.
Cowley, Malcolm. "Introduction." To *Winesburg, Ohio.*
    New York: The Viking Press, 1960, pp. 1–15.
Fagin, N. Bryllion. *The Phenomenon of Sherwood Ander-
    son.* Baltimore: The Rossi-Bryn Company, 1927.
Fanning, Michael. *France and Sherwood Anderson.* Baton
    Rouge: Louisiana State University Press, 1976.
Frank, Waldo,"Emerging Greatness." *Seven Arts* 1 (1916):
    73–78.
Geismar, Maxwell. "Sherwood Anderson: Last of the Towns-
    men." In *The Last of the Provincials.* Cambridge:
    Houghton Mifflin, 1947.
Hansen, Harry. "Sherwood Anderson: Corn-fed Mystic,
    Historian of the Middle Age of Man." In *Midwest
    Portraits.* New York: Harcourt, Brace, 1923.
Hatcher, Harlan H. "Sherwood Anderson." In *Creating the
    Modern American Novel.* New York: Farrar and Rine-
    hart, 1935.
Howe, Irving. *Sherwood Anderson.* New York: William
    Sloane Associates, 1951.
O'Brien, Edward J. "Sherwood Anderson and Waldo
    Frank." In *The Advance of the American Short Story.*
    New York: Dodd, Mead, 1923.
Parrington, Vernon L. "Sherwood Anderson: A Psycho-
    logical Naturalist." In *Main Currents in American
    Thought,* Vol 3. New York: Harcourt, Brace, 1930.
Rosenfeld, Paul. "Sherwood Anderson." In *Port of New
    York.* New York: Harcourt, Brace, 1924.
Rosenfeld, Paul. "Sherwood Anderson's Work." *Anglia*
    1 (1946): 66–88.
Schevill, James. *Sherwood Anderson: His Life and Work.*
    Denver: University of Denver Press, 1951.
Spratling, William, and William Faulkner. *Sherwood Ander-
    son and Other Famous Creoles.* New Orleans: The

Pelican Book Shop, 1926. Reprinted by The University of Texas Press: Austin and London, 1967.

Sutton, William A. *The Road to Winesburg: A Mosaic of the Imaginative Life of Sherwood Anderson.* Metuchen, New Jersey: The Scarecrow Press, 1972.

Thurston, Jarvis A. "Anderson and 'Winesburg': Mysticism and Craft." *Accent* 16(1956): 107–28.

Weber, Brom. "Sherwood Anderson and 'the Essence of Things.'" *Sewanee Review* 59(1951): 678–92.

Weber, Brom. *Sherwood Anderson.* University of Minnesota Pamphlets on American Writers No. 43. Minneapolis: University of Minnesota Press, 1964.

Index